AUTHENTIC TRANSCRIPTIONS
WITH NOTES AND TABLATURE

D1500998

Music transcriptions by Steve Gorenberg

ISBN 0-634-08410-0

HAL•LEONARD®
CORPORATION

7777 W. BLUEMOUND RD. P.O. BOX 13819 MILWAUKEE, WI 53213

Visit Hal Leonard Online at
www.halleonard.com

Last Chance

Words and Music by Chris Cester and Cameron Muncey

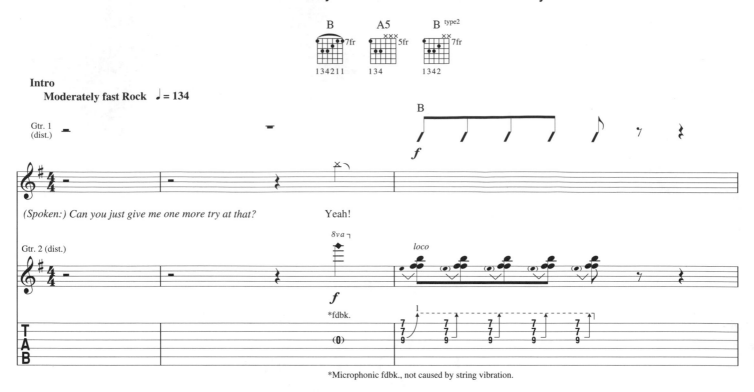

(Spoken:) Can you just give me one more try at that?

Yeah!

*Microphonic fdbk., not caused by string vibration.

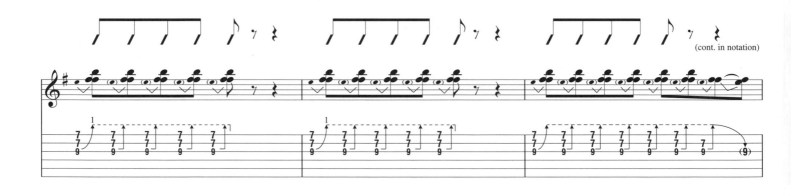

(cont. in notation)

Gtr. 1: w/ Rhy. Fig. 1

1. You ain't

Verse
Gtr. 1: w/ Rhy. Fig. 1 (1 1/2 times)

noth - ing to me ____ if you got noth - ing to say. ____
noth - ing to me, ____ so keep your hon - ey in check. ____

I don't know what you got ____ that I can use an - y - way. ____
I got some - thing for you ____ that you ain't nev-er gon - na get, ____ so come on! __

Chorus
Gtr. 2

(cont. in notation)

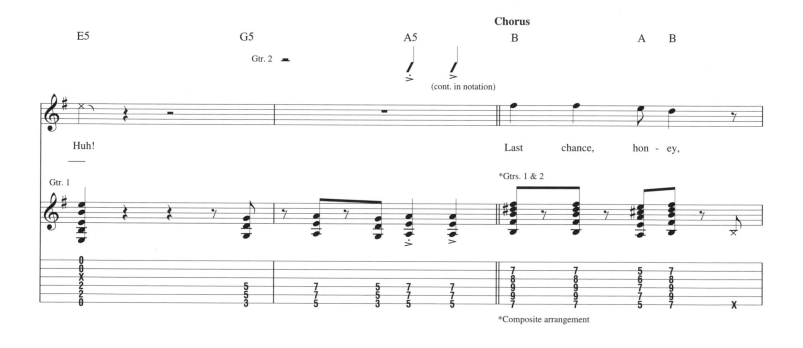

Huh!

Last chance, hon - ey,

Gtr. 1

*Gtrs. 1 & 2

*Composite arrangement

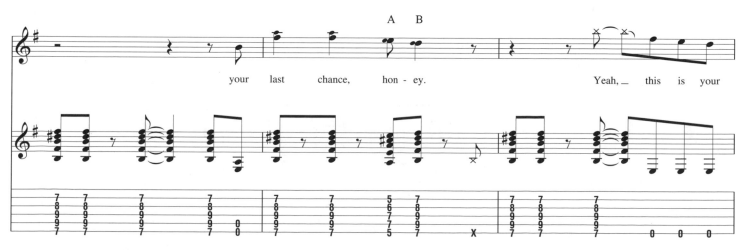

your last chance, hon - ey.

Yeah, _ this is your

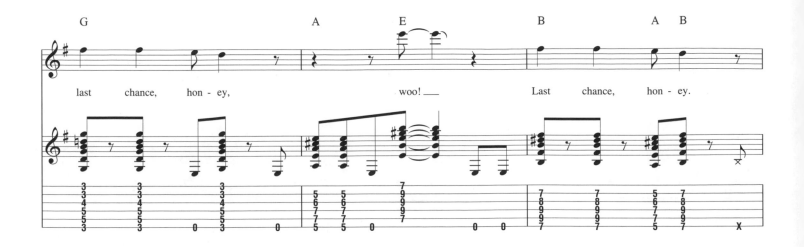

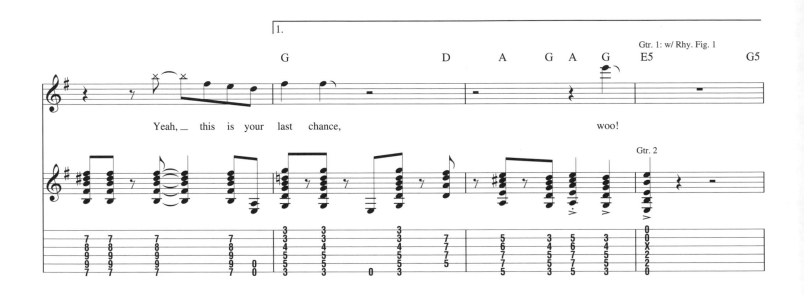

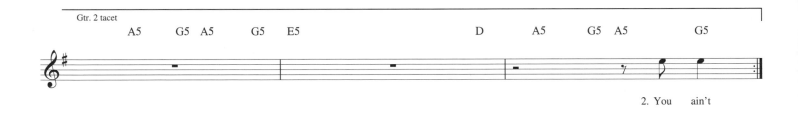

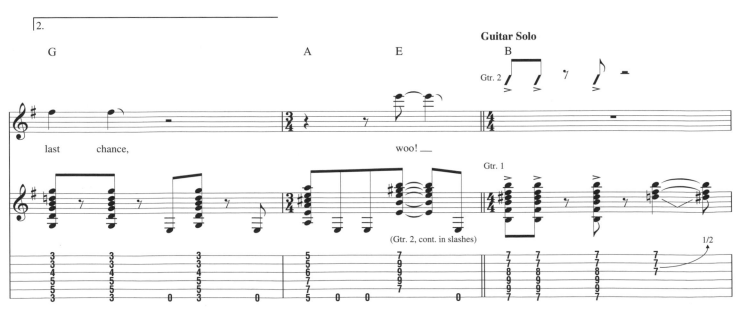

Ow.

Yeah!

(cont. in notation)

Yeah,_ this is your

Outro-Chorus

last chance, hon-ey,   woo!_   Last chance, hon-ey.

Gtrs. 1 & 2

(Gtr. 2, cont. in slashes)

B type 2

Gtr. 2

Gtr. 1

Are You Gonna Be My Girl

Words and Music by Nic Cester and Cameron Muncey

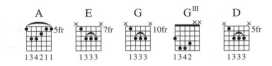

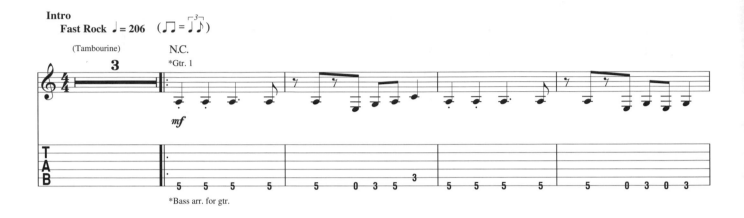

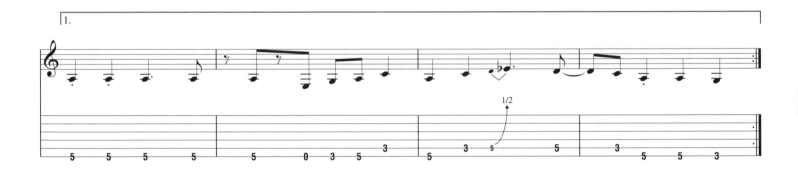

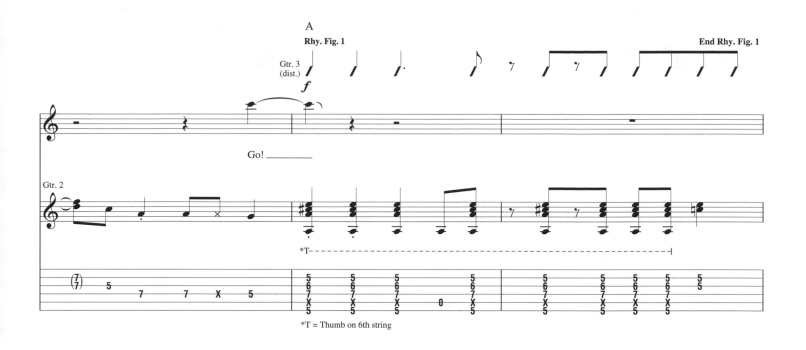

Go! _____

*T = Thumb on 6th string

Gtr. 3: w/ Rhy. Fig. 1 (2 times)

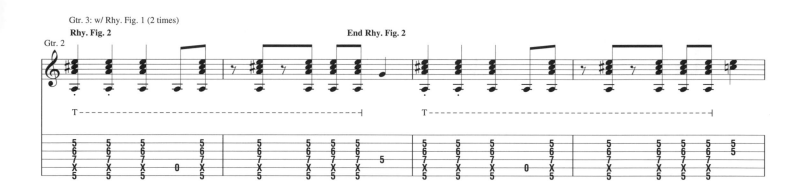

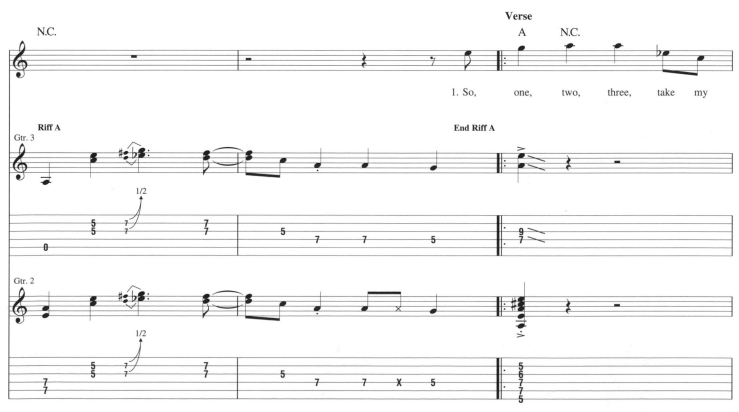

1. So,   one,   two,   three,   take   my

hand and come with me be-cause you look so fine and I real-ly want to make you mine.

I say you look so fine and I real-ly want to make you mine.

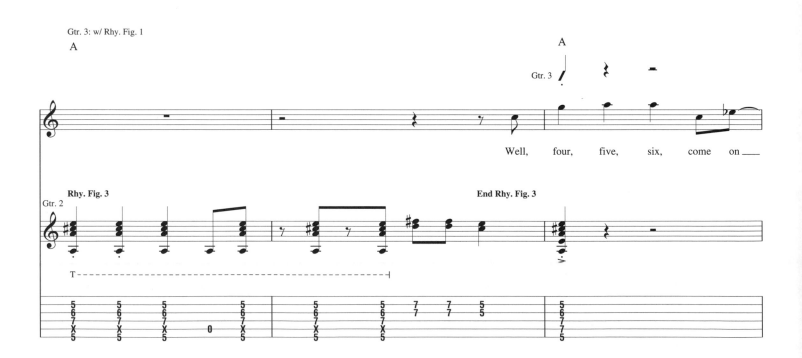

Well, four, five, six, come on ____

____ and get your kicks. Now you don't need mon-ey {when you look like that, do you, hon-ey? / with a face like that, do ya? ____}

Gtr. 3: w/ Rhy. Fig. 1

Gtr. 3: w/ Riff A

N.C.

Gtr. 2

Pre-Chorus

Gtrs. 2 & 3: w/ Rhy. Fig. 4 (2 times)

| D | C | G | D | C | G |

Big ___ black boots, long ___ brown hair. ___

Rhy. Fig. 4

End Rhy. Fig. 4

**Gtrs. 2 & 3

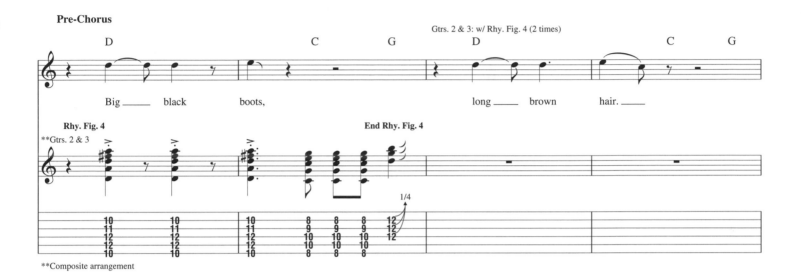

**Composite arrangement

| D | C | G | D |

She's ___ so sweet with ___ her get ___ back stare.

Gtrs. 2 & 3

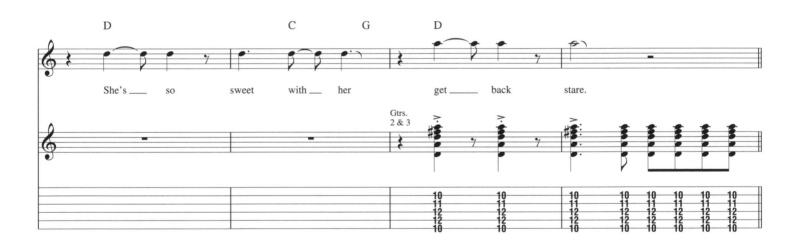

Chorus

| A | C |

Well, I could see ___ you home with me, ___

Rhy. Fig. 5

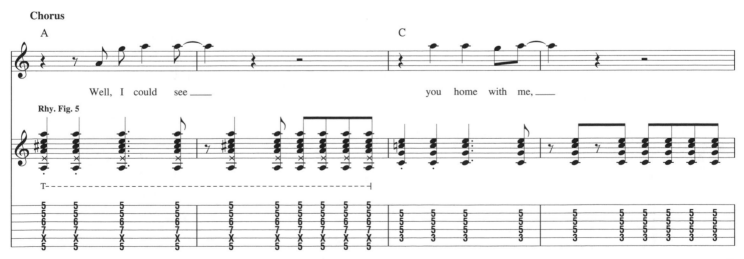

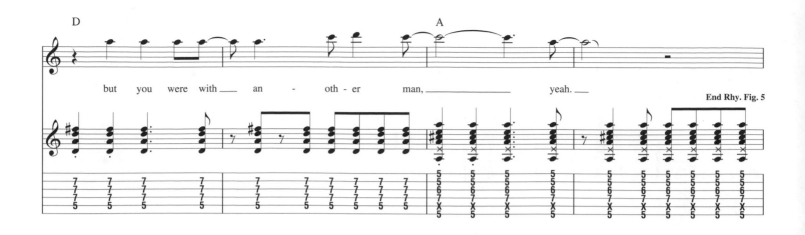

but you were with ___ an - oth - er man, _____ yeah. ___

End Rhy. Fig. 5

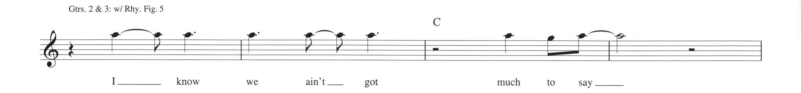

Gtrs. 2 & 3: w/ Rhy. Fig. 5

I _____ know we ain't ___ got much to say ___

be - fore I let _____ you get a - way, _____ yeah. ___

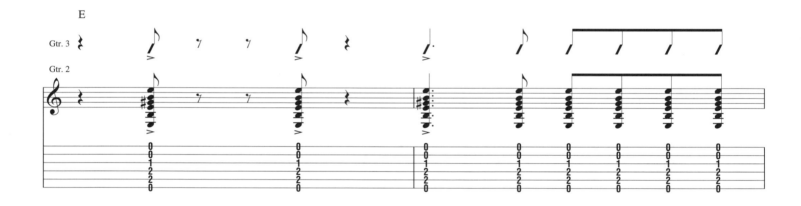

Gtr. 3

Gtr. 2

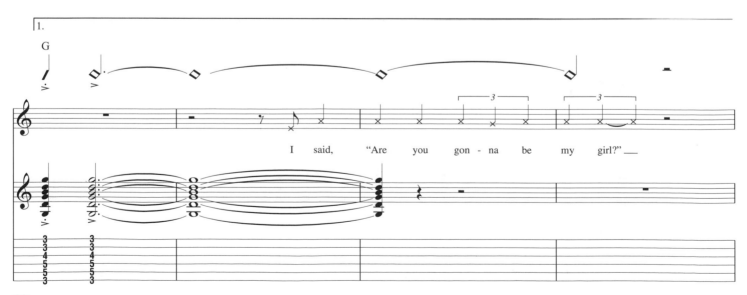

1.

I said, "Are you gon - na be my girl?" ___

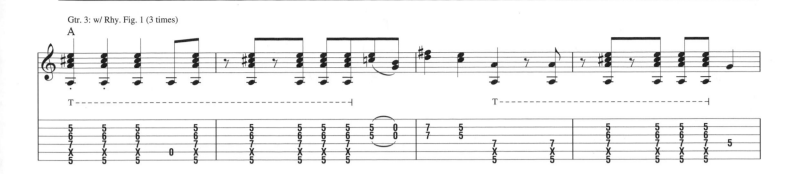

Gtr. 3: w/ Rhy. Fig. 1 (3 times)

A

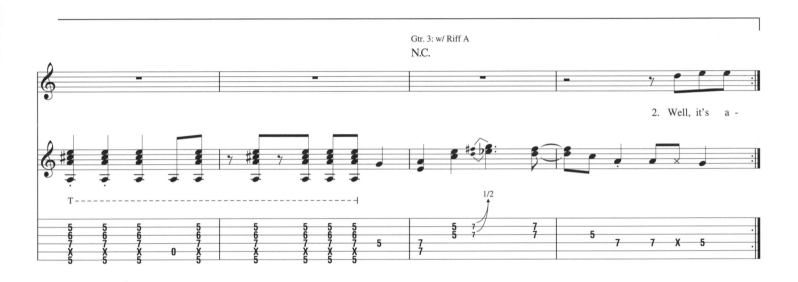

Gtr. 3: w/ Riff A

N.C.

2. Well, it's a-

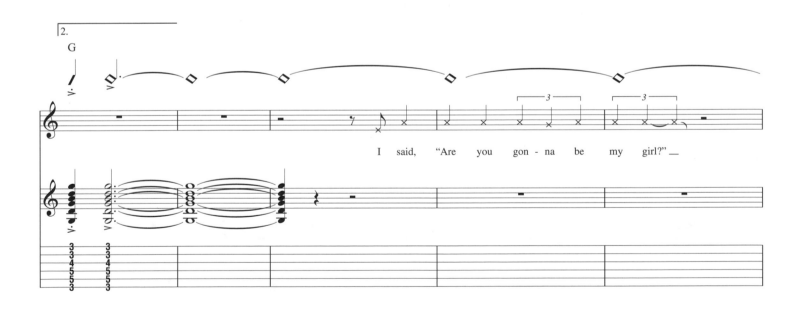

2.

G

I said, "Are you gon-na be my girl?"—

Gtr. 2: w/ Rhy. Fig. 2 (4 times)

Gtr. 3 tacet

A5

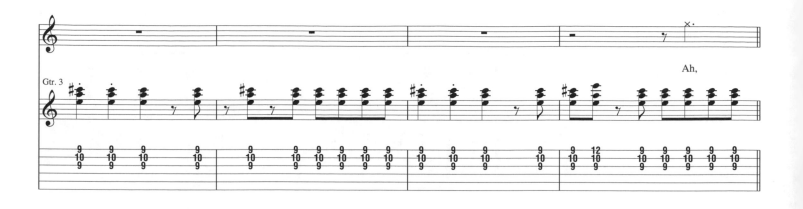

Ah,

Guitar Solo
Gtr. 2: w/ Rhy. Fig. 2 (4 times)

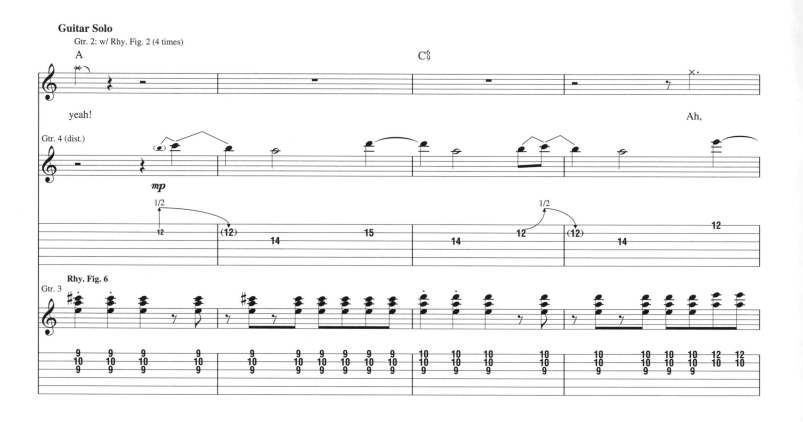

yeah!

Ah,

Rhy. Fig. 6

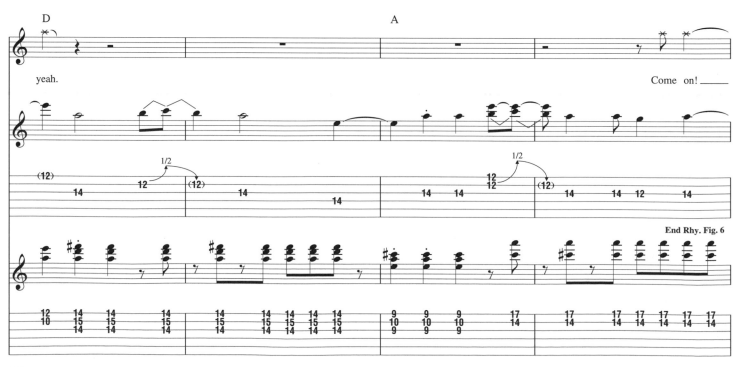

yeah.

Come on! _____

End Rhy. Fig. 6

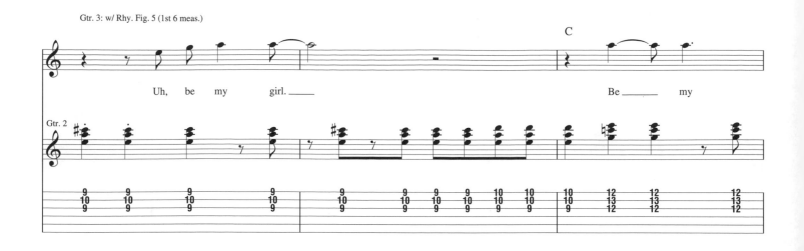

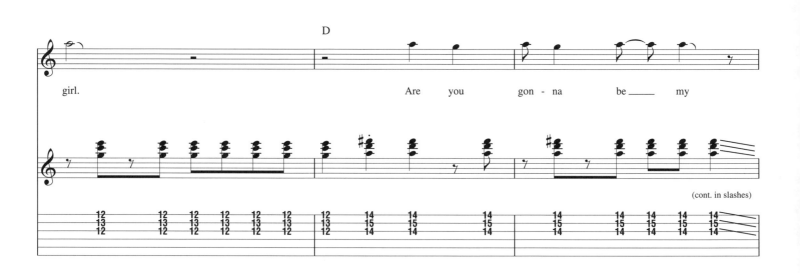

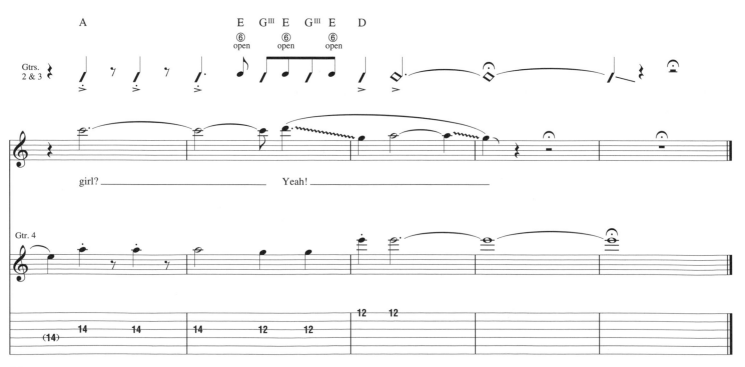

14

Rollover D.J.

Words and Music by Nic Cester and Cameron Muncey

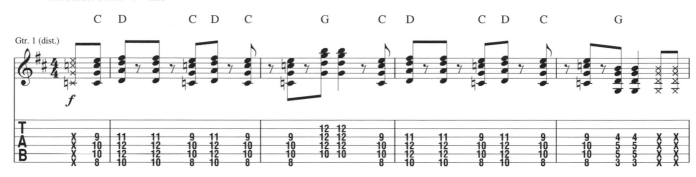

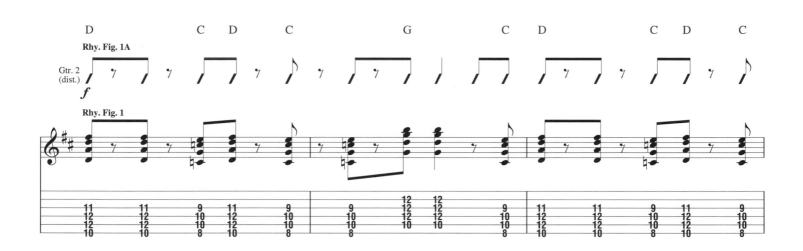

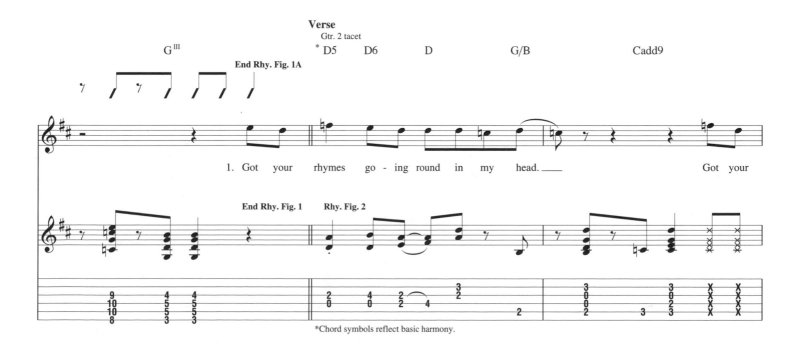

*Chord symbols reflect basic harmony.

su - per - son - ic beats mix - ing up my Keds. __ So dance, lit - tle D. J., come on. __

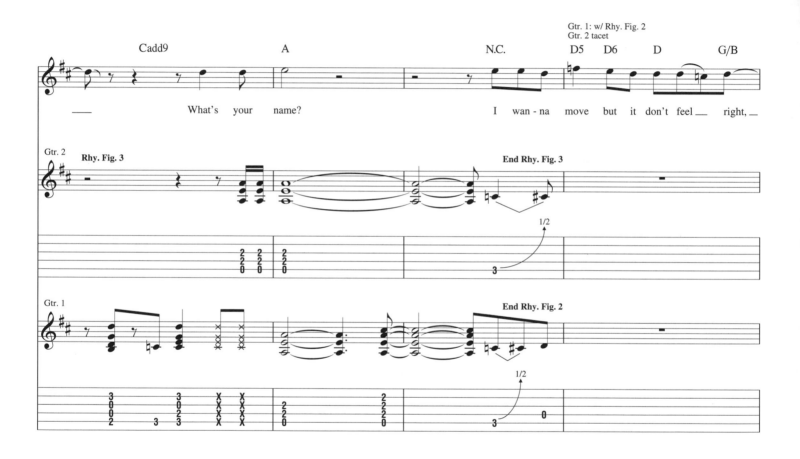

__ What's your name? I wan - na move but it don't feel __ right, __

'cause you've been play - ing oth - er peo - ple's songs __ all night. __ So

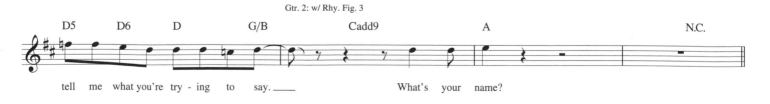

tell me what you're try - ing to say. ___ What's your name?

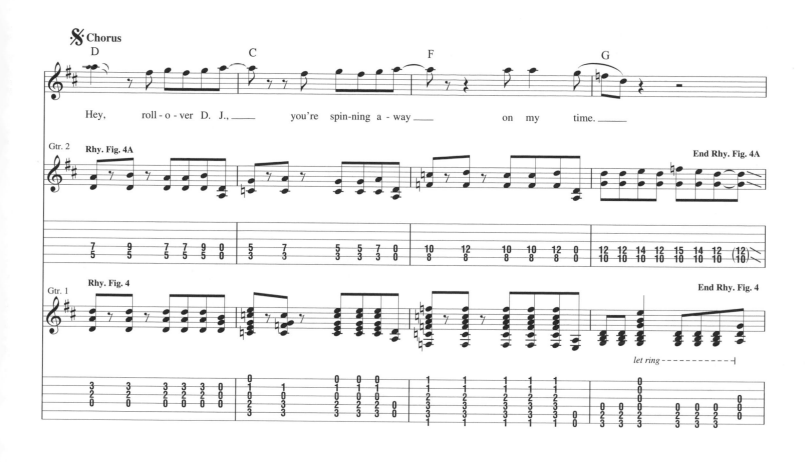

% Chorus

Hey, roll-o-ver D. J., _____ you're spin-ning a-way _____ on my time. _____

Gtr. 2

Rhy. Fig. 4A

End Rhy. Fig. 4A

Gtr. 1

Rhy. Fig. 4

End Rhy. Fig. 4

let ring - - - - - - - - - - - -|

Gtrs. 1 & 2: w/ Rhy. Figs. 4 & 4A

Hey, who cares what you play? ____ Say what-ev-er you say, ____ 'cause I don't mind. _____

To Coda ⊕

Hey, roll-o-ver D. J., _____ if you don't mind. _____

Gtr. 2

Gtr. 1

2. Well, I know that you think you're a star. ___

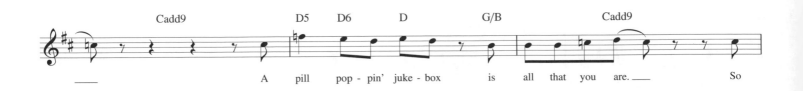

___ A pill pop-pin' juke-box is all that you are. ___ So

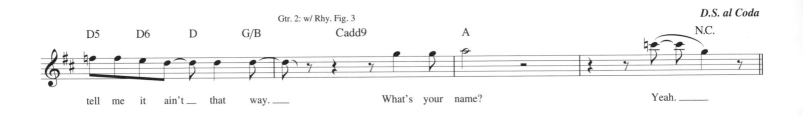

tell me it ain't ___ that way. ___ What's your name? Yeah. _____

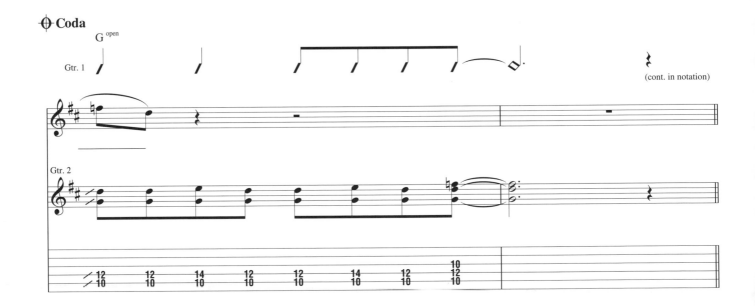

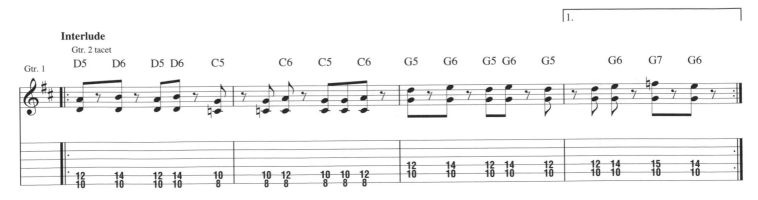

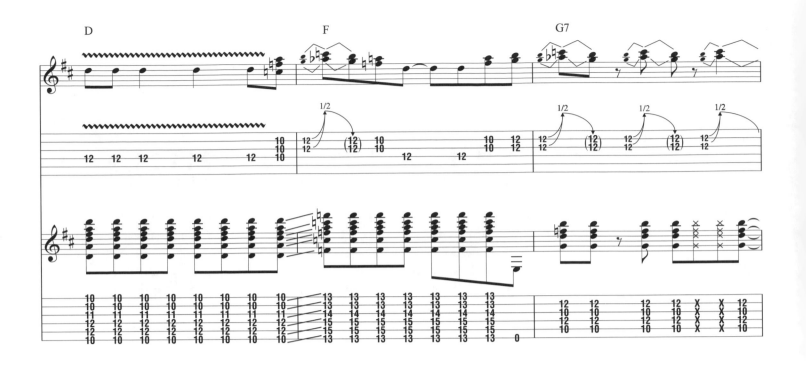

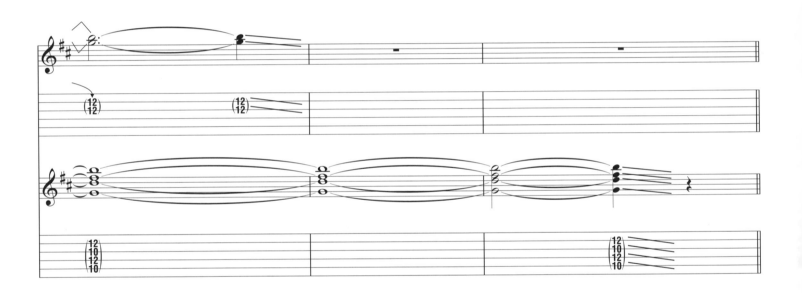

Chorus
Gtrs. 1 & 2: w/ Rhy. Figs. 4 & 4A (2 times)

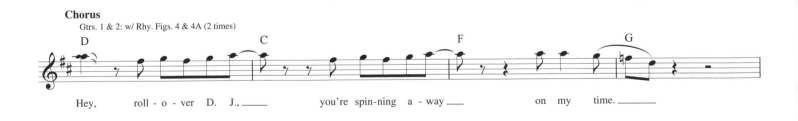

Hey,   roll - o - ver D. J.,____   you're spin-ning a - way____   on my time.____

Hey,   who cares what you play?____   Say what-ev - er you say,____   'cause I don't mind.____

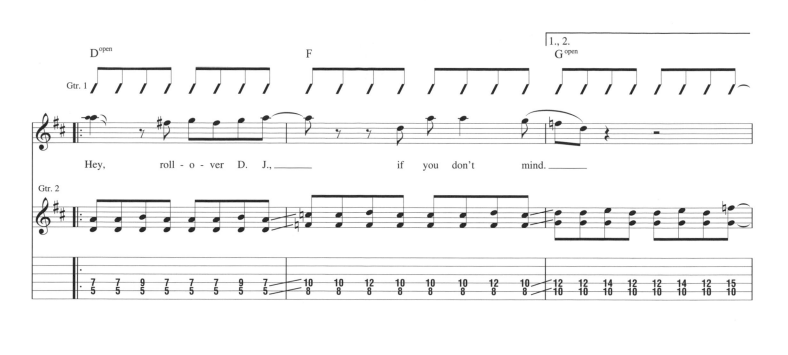

Hey, roll - o - ver D. J., _____ if you don't mind. _____

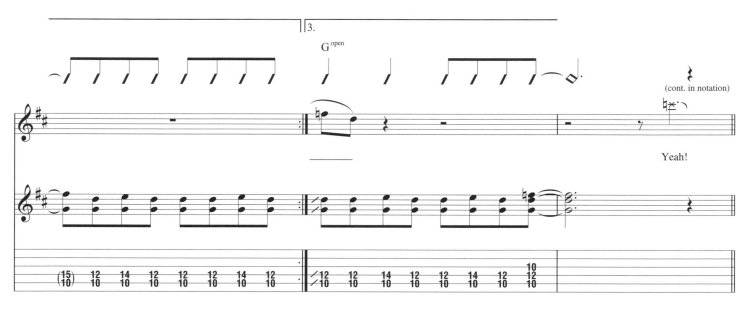

Yeah!

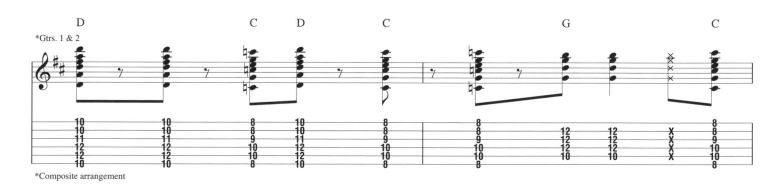

*Gtrs. 1 & 2

*Composite arrangement

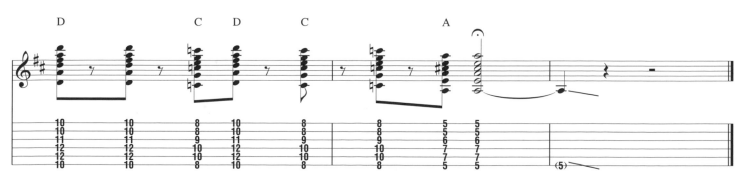

Look What You've Done

Words and Music by Nic Cester

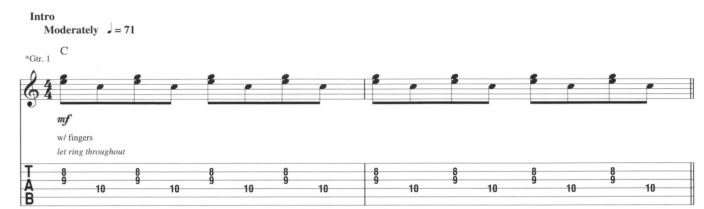

Intro
Moderately ♩ = 71

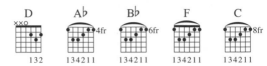

*Gtr. 1

*Piano arr. for gtr.

𝄋 Verse

2nd time, Gtrs. 2 & 3 tacet
3rd time, Gtrs. 2 & 3: w/ Rhy. Fill 1

1. Take my pho - to off the wall _____ if it _____ just _____ won't sing _____ for you _____
2. Give me back my point of view _____ 'cause I _____ just _____ can't think _____ for you. _____
3. Take my pho - to off the wall _____ if it _____ just _____ won't sing _____ for you _____

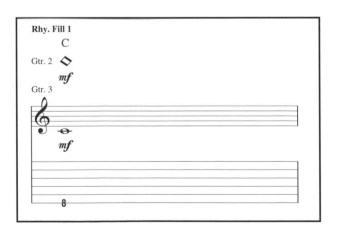

Rhy. Fill 1

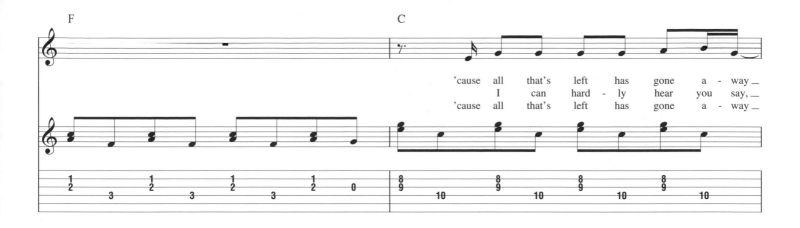

'cause all that's left has gone a - way __
I can hard - ly hear you say, __
'cause all that's left has gone a - way __

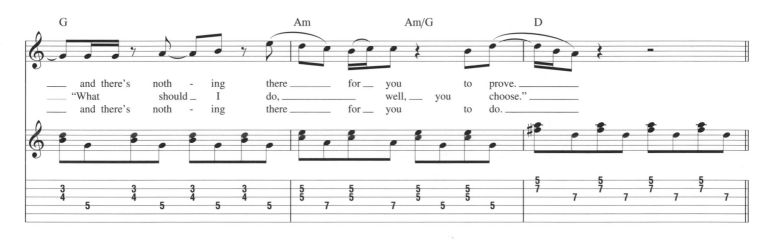

__ and there's noth - ing there _____ for __ you to prove. ___
__ "What should __ I do, _____ well, __ you choose." ___
__ and there's noth - ing there _____ for __ you to do. ___

Chorus

Oh, look what you've done, __ you've made __ a fool __ of __ ev - 'ry - one. ___

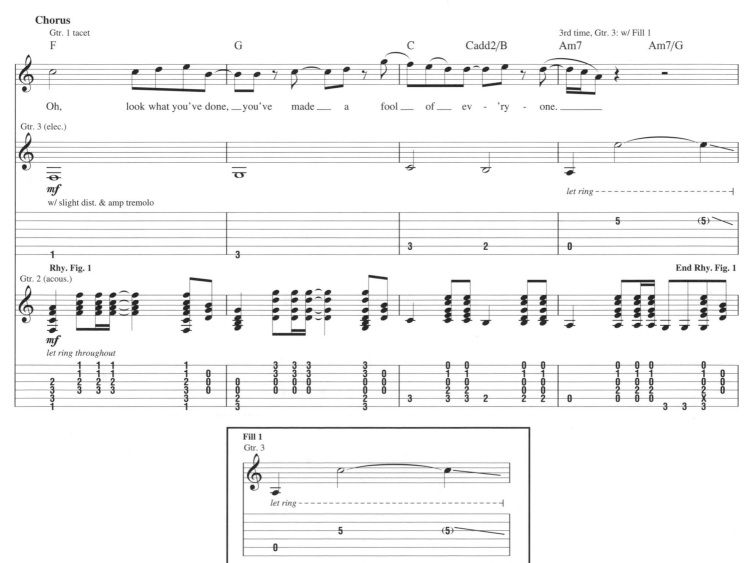

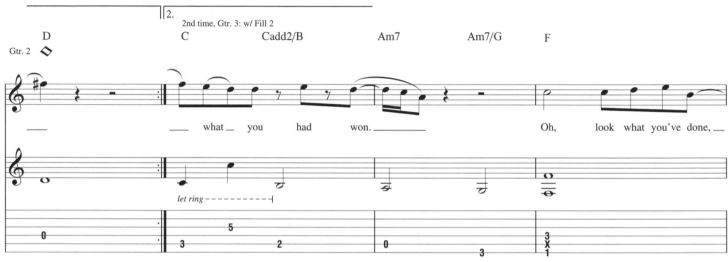

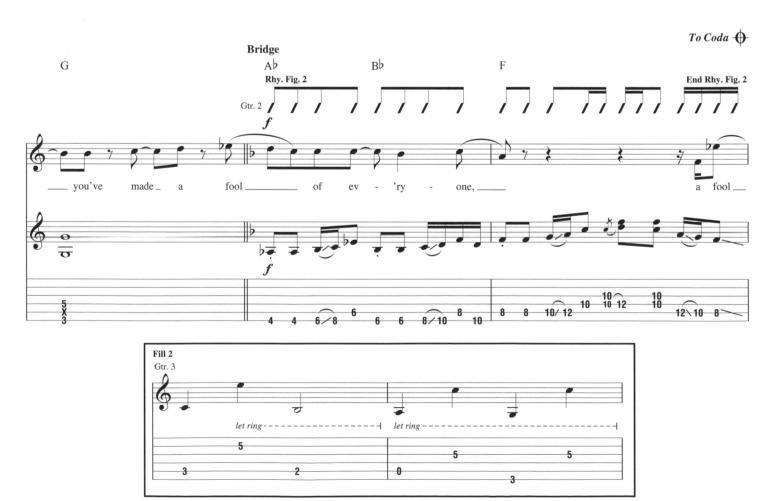

Coda

Outro

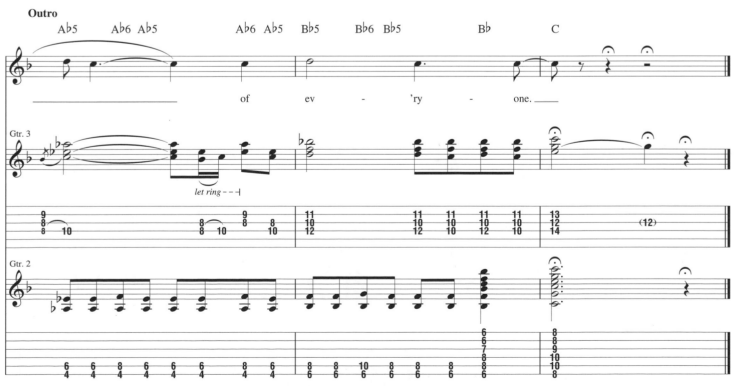

Get What You Need

Words and Music by Nic Cester, Chris Cester and Cameron Muncey

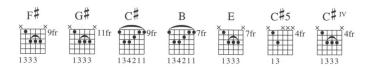

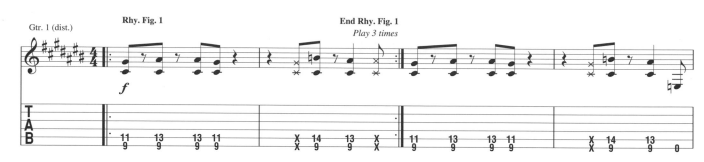

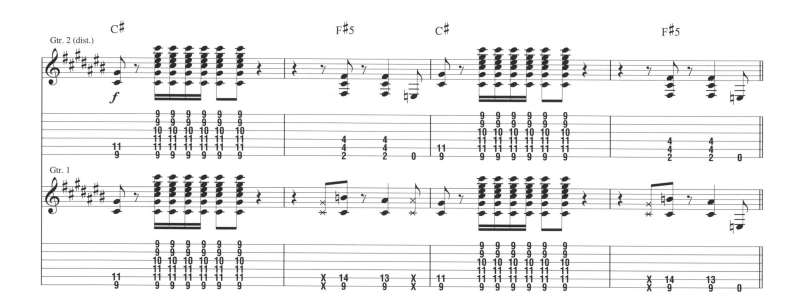

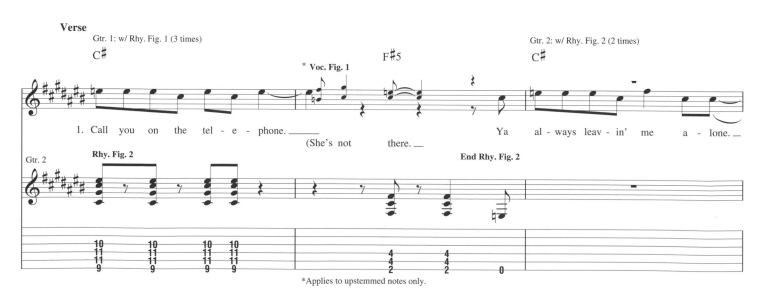

*Applies to upstemmed notes only.

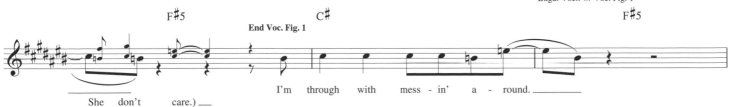

She don't care.) I'm through with mess-in' a-round.

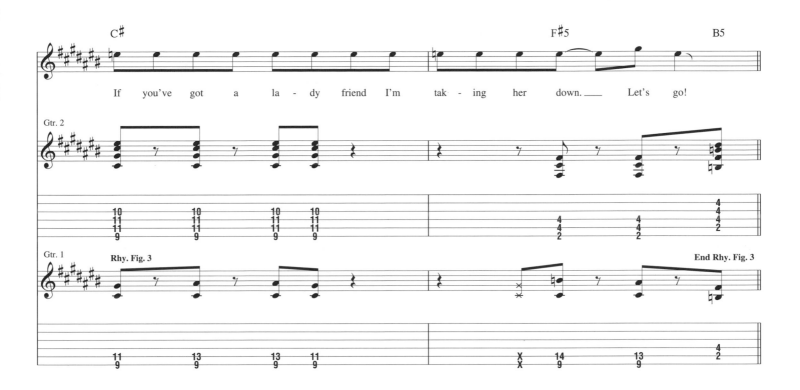

If you've got a la-dy friend I'm tak-ing her down. Let's go!

⅌ Pre-Chorus

So come on. Yeah, come on.

**(Yeah!)

*Composite arrangement

**2nd time only.

Come on.

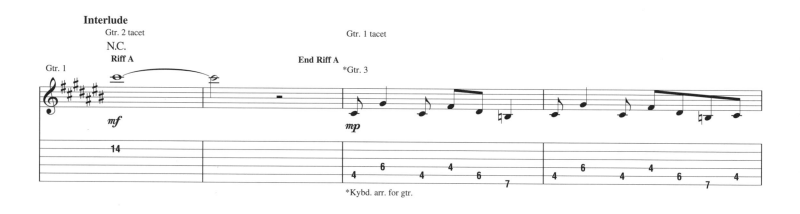

28

Chorus

Gtr. 3 tacet

Gtrs. 1 & 2: w/ Rhy. Figs. 5 & 5A (2 1/2 times)

get what you need. __
(Gon - na get what you need. __
You're gon - na get what you need. __
Gon - na

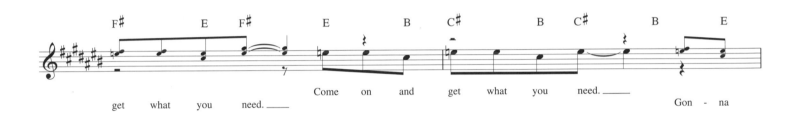

Come on and get what you need. ____
get what you need. ____
Gon - na

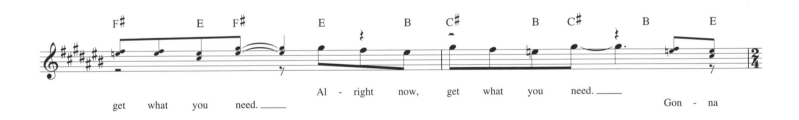

Al - right now, get what you need. ____
get what you need. ____
Gon - na

To Coda ⊕

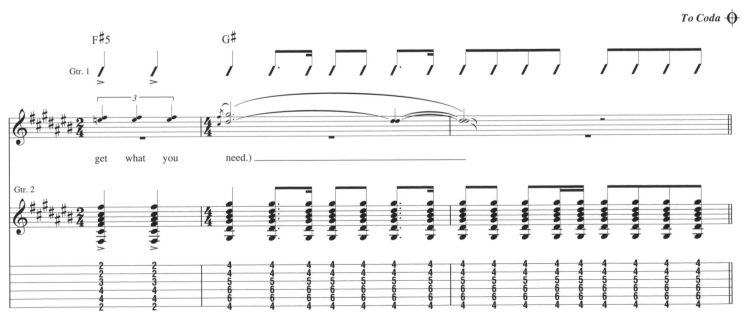

get what you need.) _____

Interlude

Gtr. 1: w/ Riff A
Gtr. 2 tacet

N.C.

Verse

N.C.

2. Now I'm in a rock-in' band. _____
(She's not there.) _
No one has to hold my hand. _

D.S. al Coda

Gtrs. 1 & 2: w/ Rhy. Figs. 1 & 2   Gtr. 1: w/ Rhy. Fig. 3

C#   F#5   C#   F#5   B5

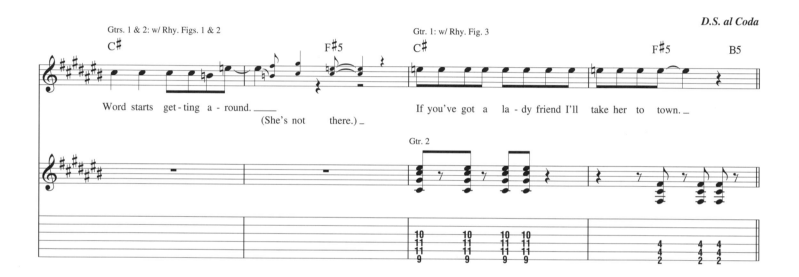

Word starts get-ting a-round. _____
(She's not there.) _
If you've got a la-dy friend I'll take her to town. _

Gtr. 2

⊕ Coda

Interlude

Gtr. 1: w/ Riff A
Gtr. 2 tacet

N.C.

C#5   C#6 C#5

Gtr. 4 (dist.)

Rhy. Fig. 6

mf

C#6 C#5   C#6 C#5   N.C.   A5   B5 C#5

End Rhy. Fig. 6

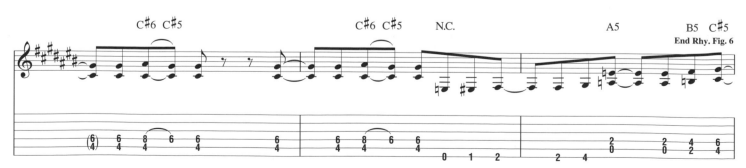

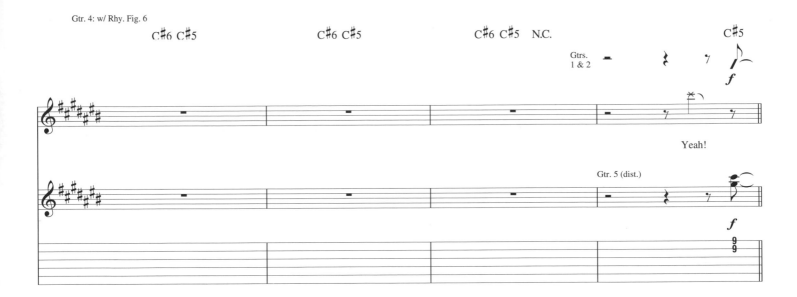

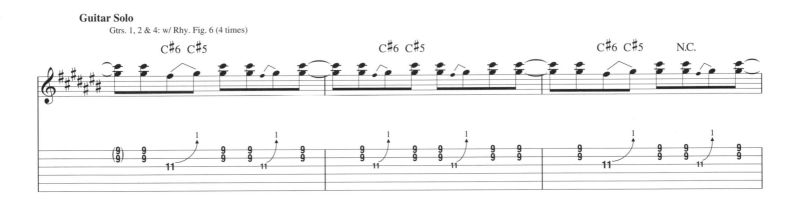

Guitar Solo

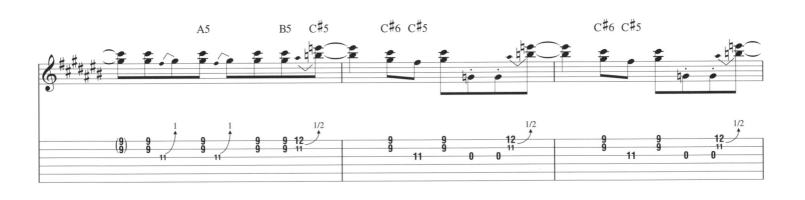

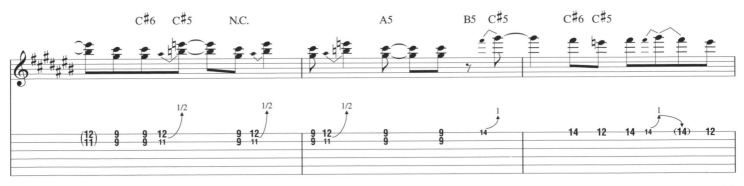

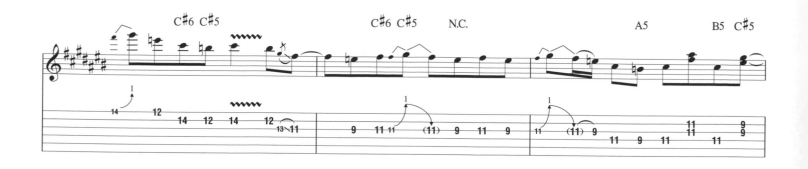

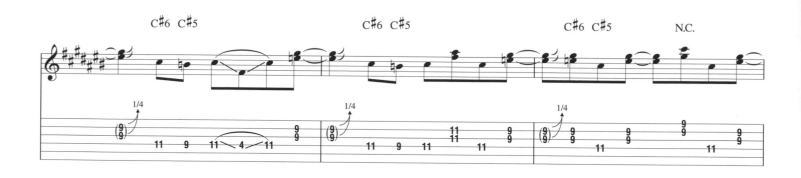

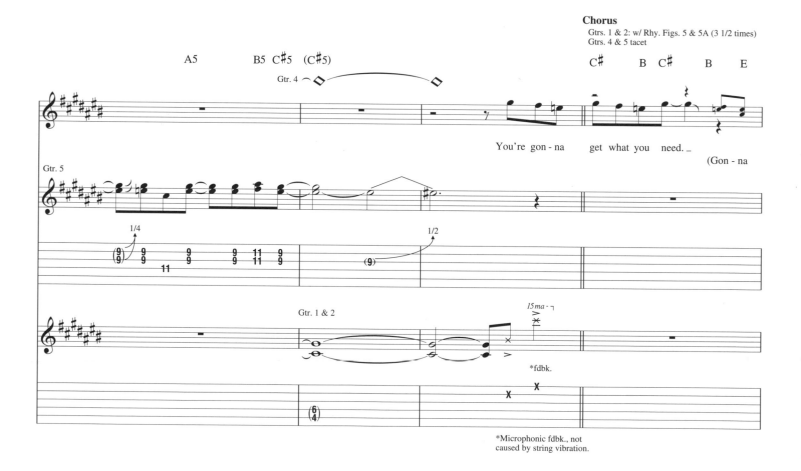

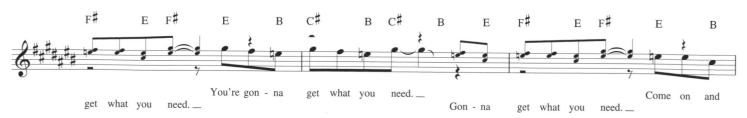

get what you need. ___
Gon - na   get what you need. ___   You're gon - na   get what you need. ___   Gon - na

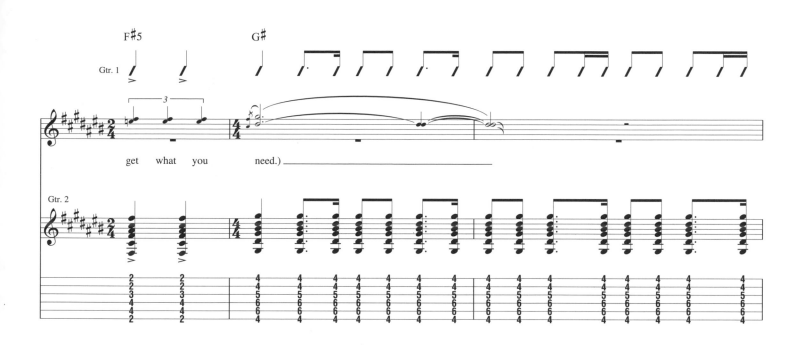

get what you need.) _____

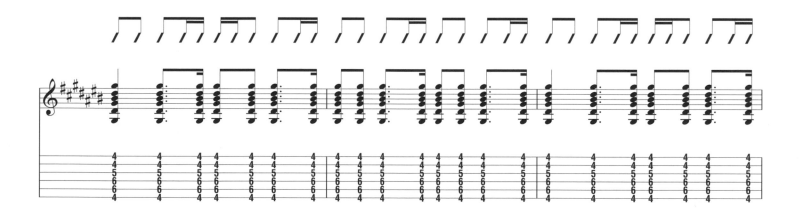

Free time

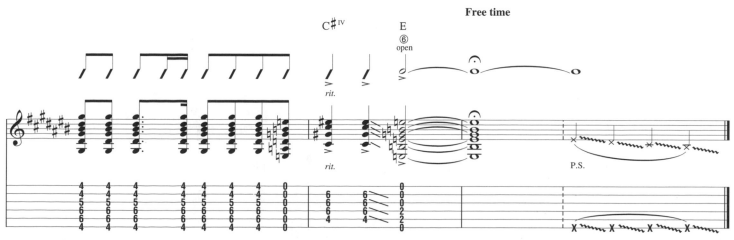

Move On

Words and Music by Nic Cester and Chris Cester

Gtr. 1: Capo III
Gtrs. 3, 4 & 5: Open G tuning:
(low to high) D-G-D-G-B-D

Intro
Free time

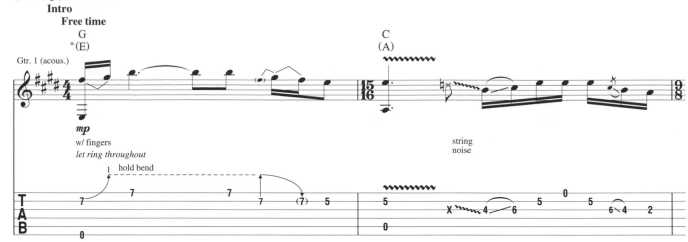

*Symbols in parentheses represent chord names respective to capoed guitar.
Symbols above reflect actual saounding chords (implied harmony). Capoed
fret is "0" in tab.

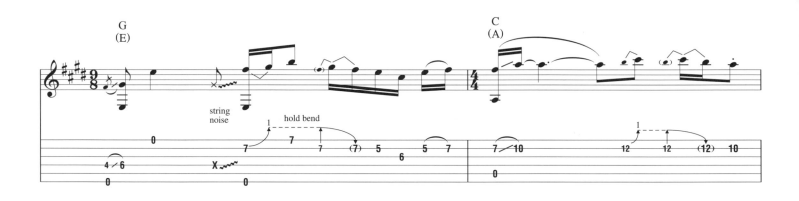

Slow ♩ = 60

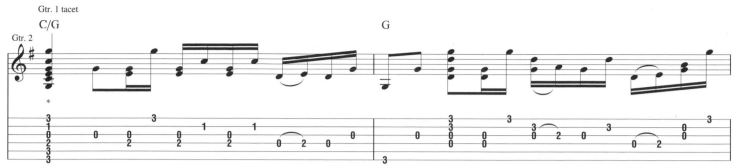

Gtr. 1 tacet

Gtr. 2

*Fret 5th & 6th strings w/ 3rd finger.

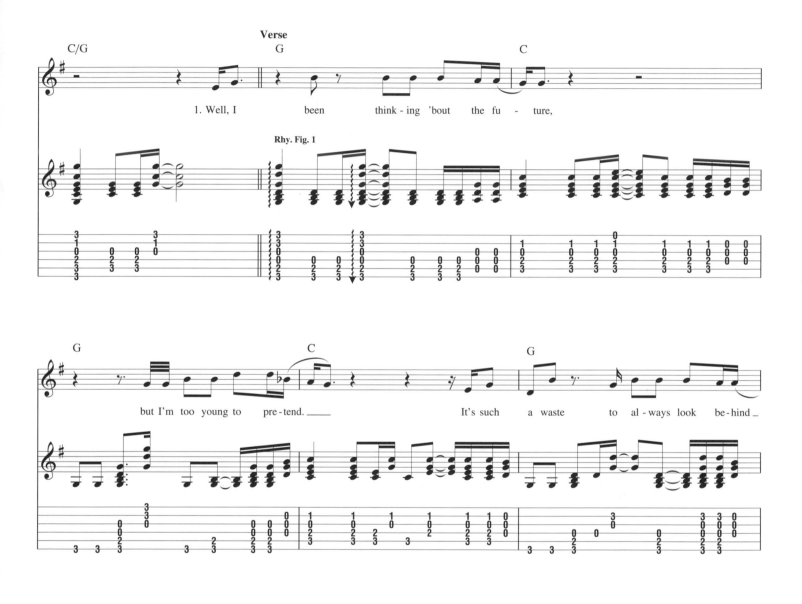

Verse

1. Well, I been think-ing 'bout the fu-ture,

Rhy. Fig. 1

but I'm too young to pre-tend. _____ It's such a waste to al-ways look be-hind _____

_____ you, _____ you should be look-in' straight a-head. _____

End Rhy. Fig. 1

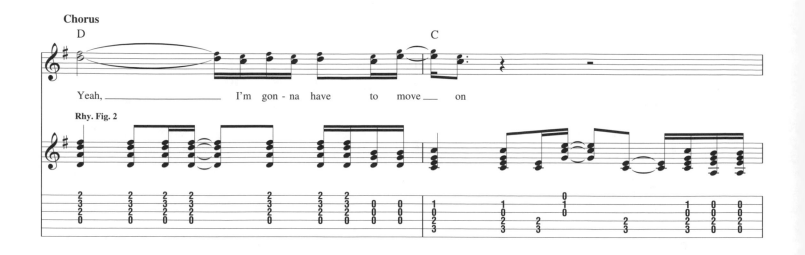

Chorus

Yeah, _____ I'm gon-na have to move___ on

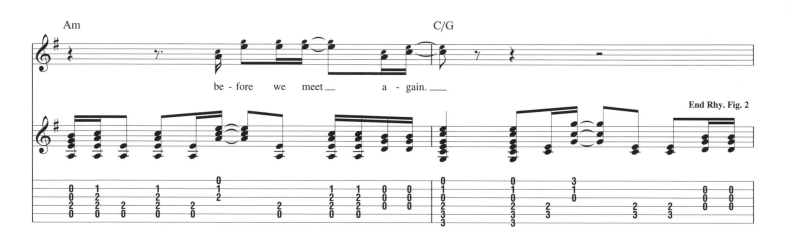

be - fore we meet___ a - gain. ___

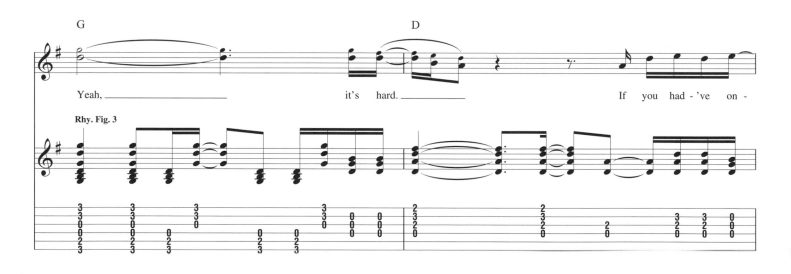

Yeah, _____ it's hard._____ If you had - 've on -

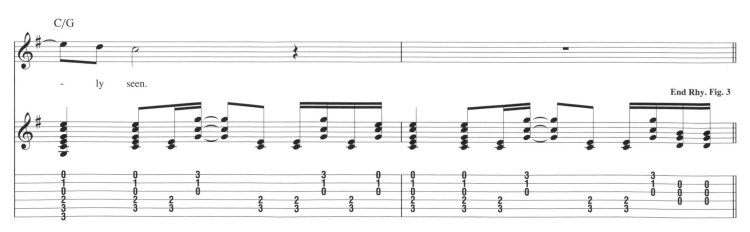

- ly seen.

Interlude

Verse

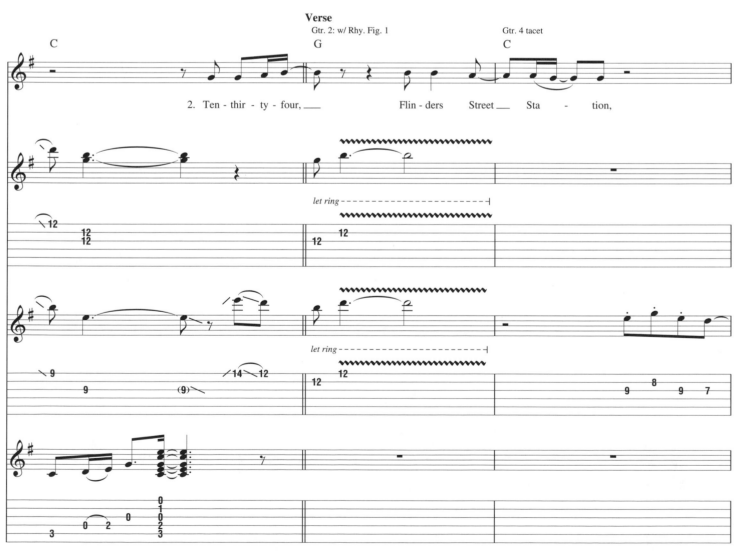

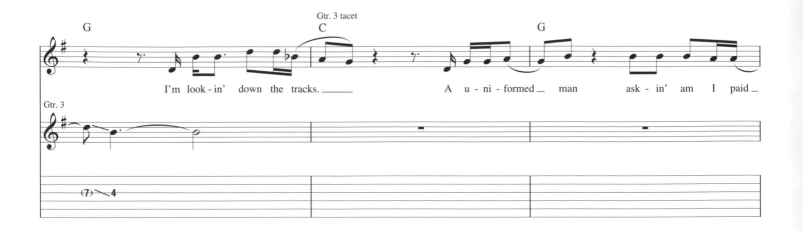

I'm look-in' down the tracks. _____ A u-ni-formed _____ man ask-in' am I paid _____

_____ up. Why would I wan-na be _____ that? _____

Chorus

Gtr. 2: w/ Rhy. Fig. 2

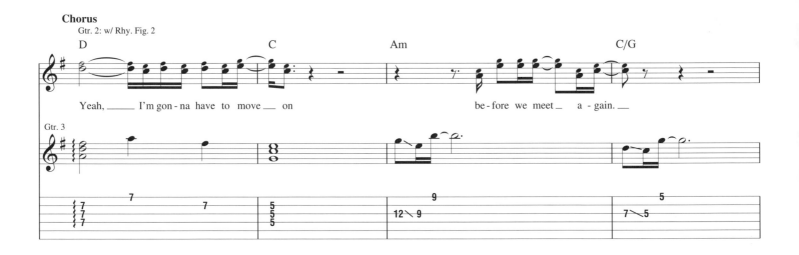

Yeah, _____ I'm gon-na have to move _____ on be-fore we meet _____ a-gain. _____

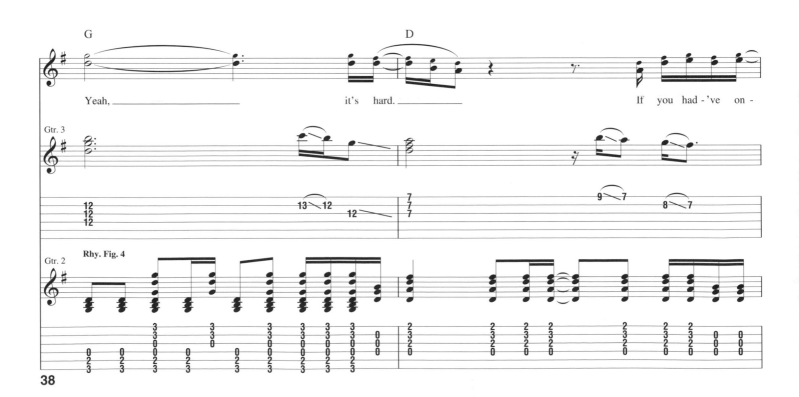

Yeah, _____ it's hard. _____ If you had-'ve on-

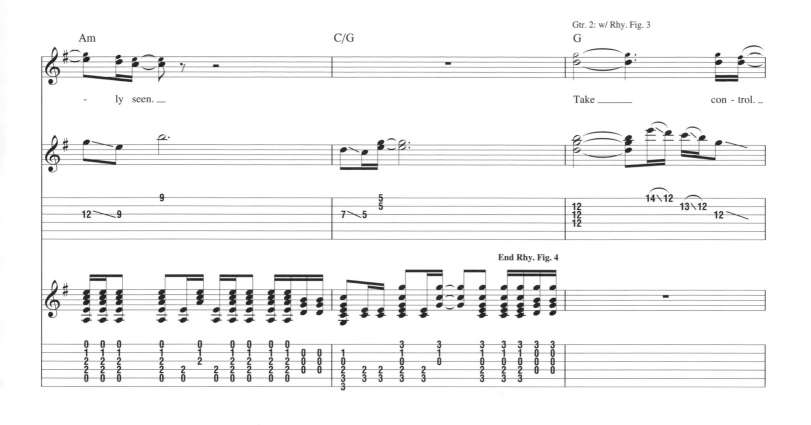

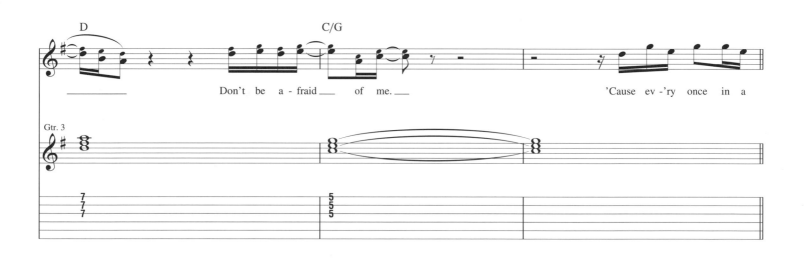

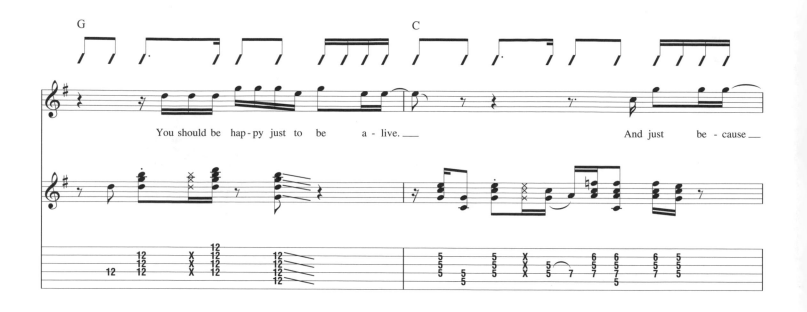

You should be hap-py just to be a - live. ___ And just be - cause ___

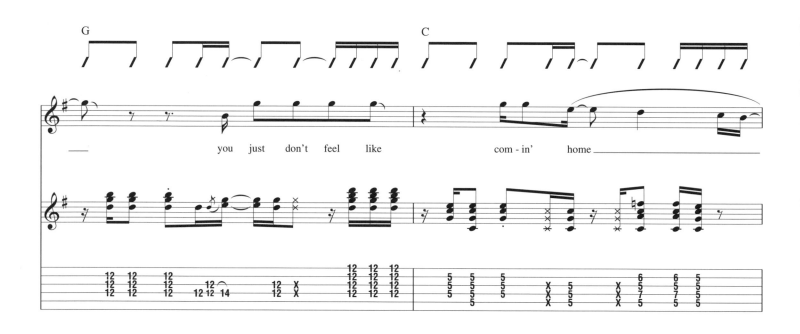

___ you just don't feel like com - in' home ___

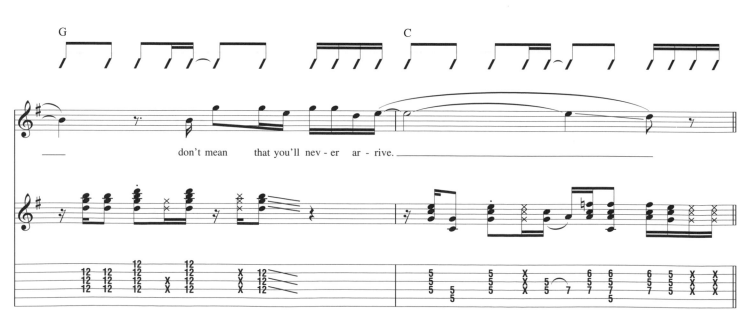

___ don't mean that you'll nev - er ar - rive. ___

Chorus
Gtr. 2: w/ Rhy. Fig. 2
Gtr. 5 tacet

41

Radio Song

Words and Music by Nic Cester, Chris Cester and Cameron Muncey

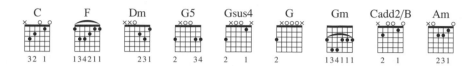

Verse

2nd time, Gtrs. 4 & 5: w/ Rhy. Fills 1 & 1A

1. Take a look ___ at what I took, ___ a
you all know ___ of the em - per - or's clothes ___

leaf out ___ of ev - 'ry - bod - y's ___ book. ___ We see ___ what
walk - ing ___ down an emp - ty ___ road. ___ We see ___ what

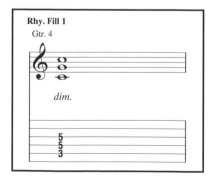

you _____ can't see. _____ I'm caught in a trap of my own, __
you _____ can't see. _____ That's not how I wan-na be. __

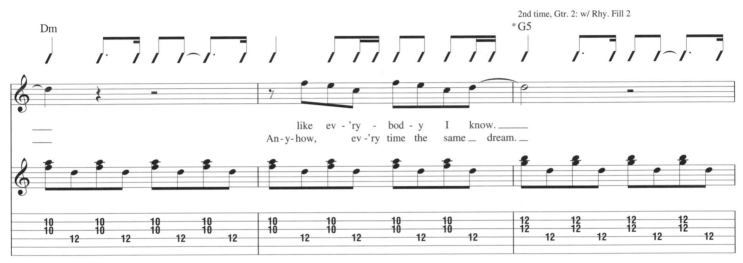

_____ like ev-'ry-bod-y I know. __
An-y-how, ev-'ry time the same __ dream. __

*2nd time, Gtr. 1 plays G.

Chorus

This won't be played __ on your ra-di-o __ to-night. __

Riff A
Gtr. 3 (elec.)

f
w/ fuzz & **gated amp tremolo
grad. bend

**Tremolo set for sixteenth-note regeneration.

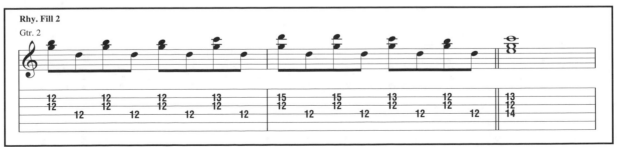

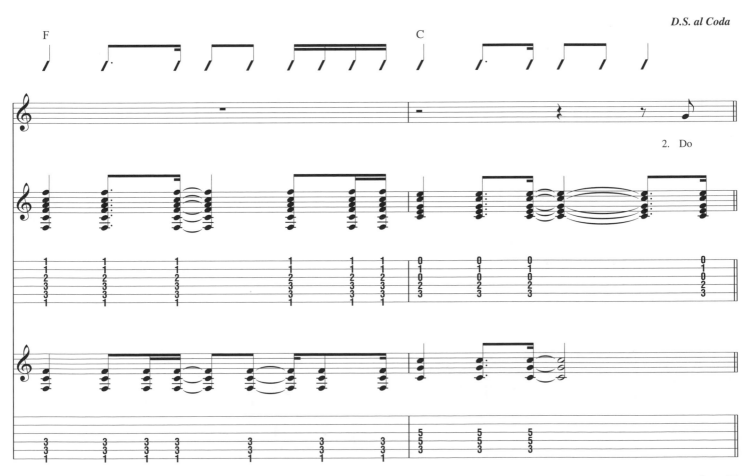

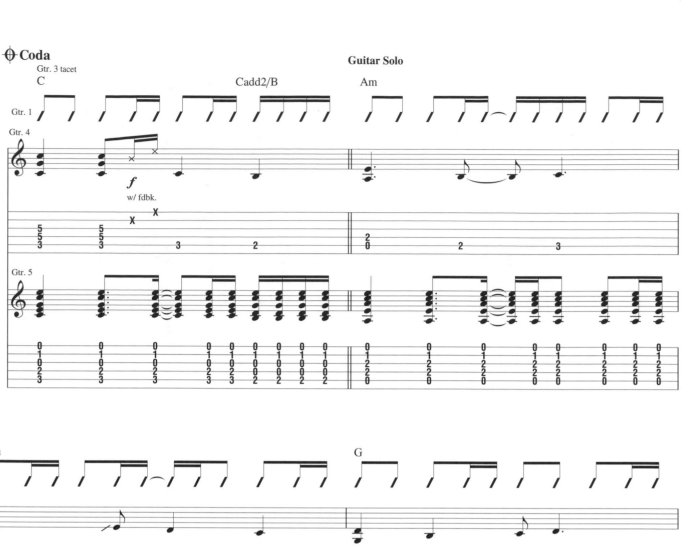

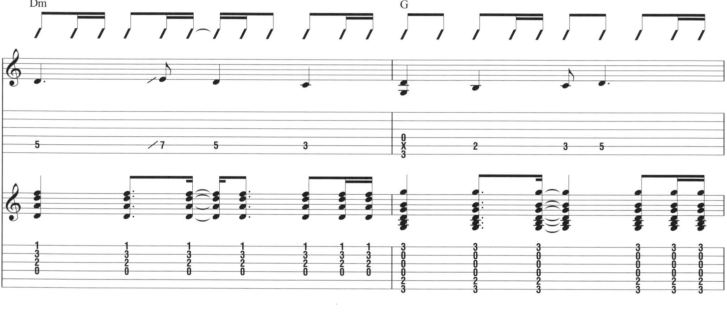

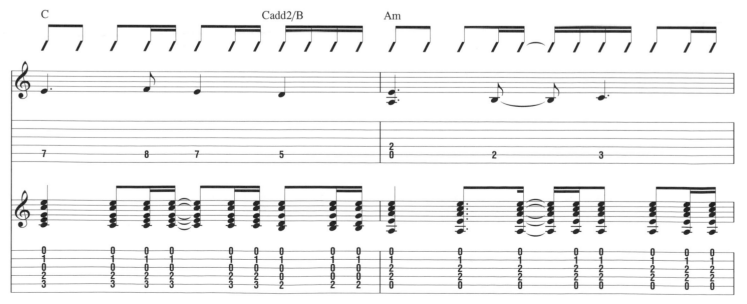

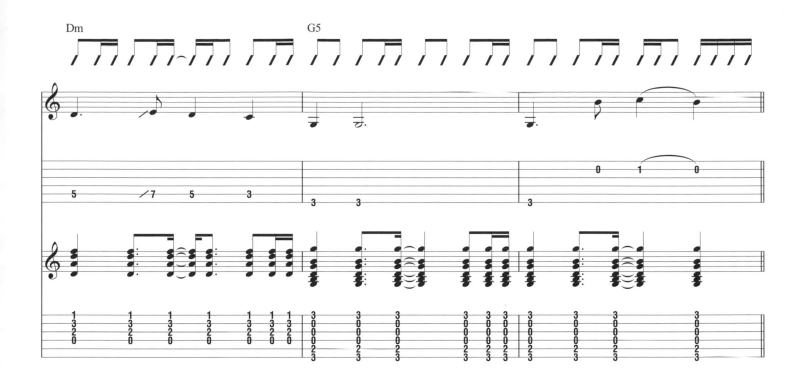

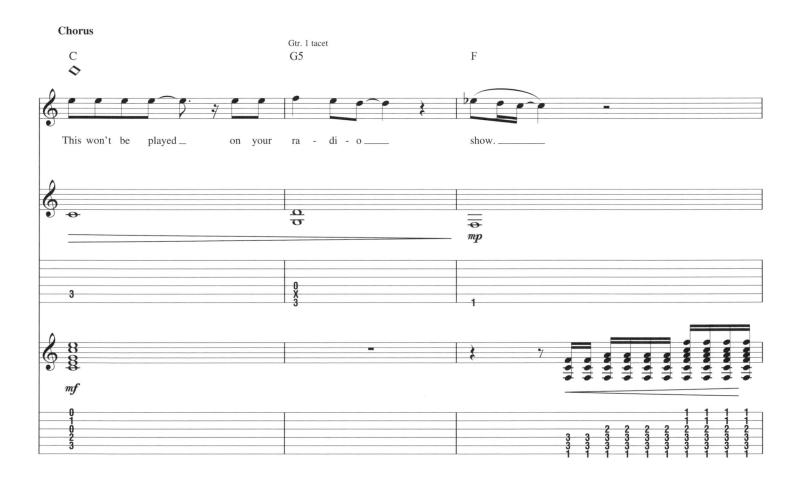

Chorus

This won't be played ___ on your ra - di - o ___ show. ___

Gtrs. 1, 4 & 5: w/ Rhy. Figs. 1, 1A & 1B (last meas.)   Gtrs. 1, 4 & 5: w/ Rhy. Figs. 2, 2A & 2B   Gtr. 3: w/ Riff A

This won't be played ___ on your ra - di - o ___ to - night. ___

Gtrs. 1, 4 & 5: w/ Rhy. Figs. 1, 1A & 1B

Oh,   no.

Outro

Gtrs. 1, 4 & 5: w/ Rhy. Figs. 1, 1A & 1B (2 1/2 times)

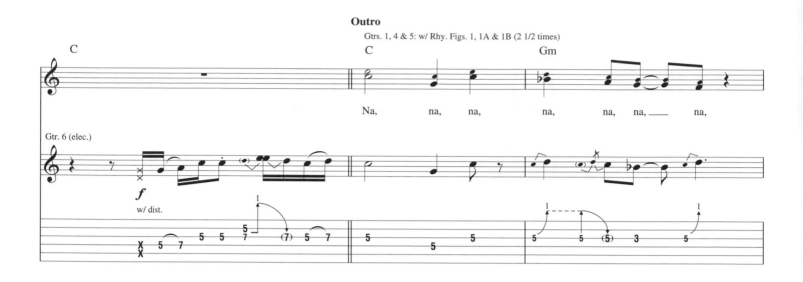

Na,   na,   na,   na,   na,   na,   na,

Gtr. 6 (elec.)

f

w/ dist.

na,   na,   na,   na,   na,   na,   na.   Na,   na,   na,

na,   na,   na,   na,   na,   na,   na,   na,   na,   na.

Na, na, na, na, na, na, na,

na, na, na, na, na.

Get Me Outta Here

Words and Music by Nic Cester and Chris Cester

A

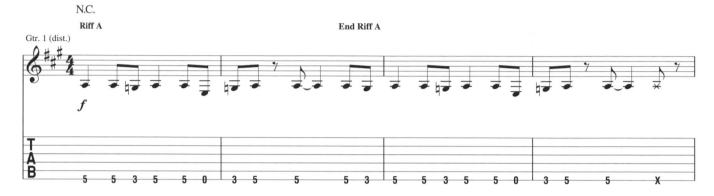

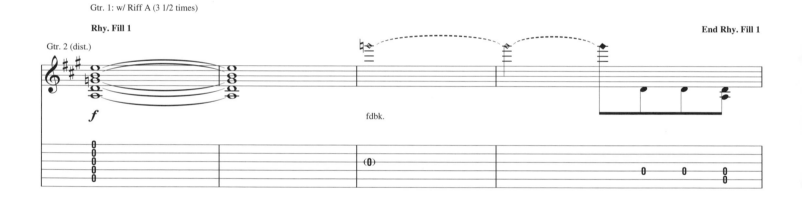

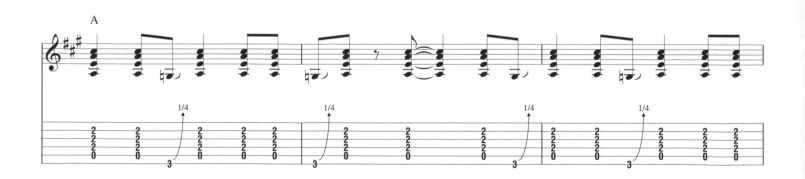

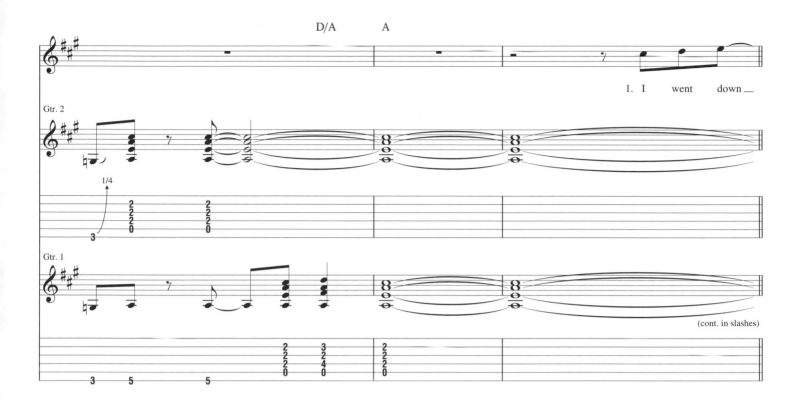

D/A   A

1. I went down __

Gtr. 2

1/4

Gtr. 1

(cont. in slashes)

Verse

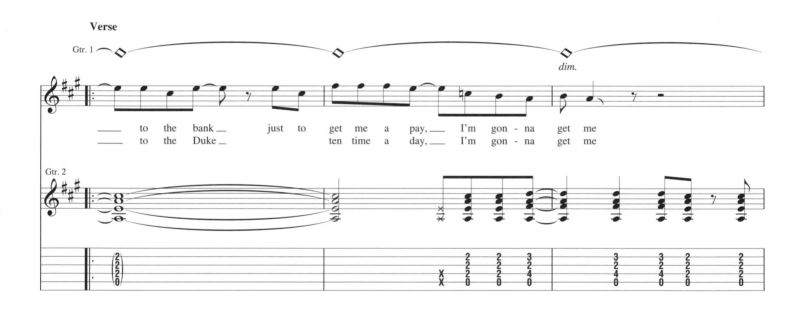

Gtr. 1

dim.

__ to the bank __ just to get me a pay, __ I'm gon - na get me
__ to the Duke __ ten time a day, __ I'm gon - na get me

Gtr. 2

Gtr. 1 tacet

A   D/A

out - ta here. __   I got me some cash, __ I'm head - ing back to L. A., __ I'm gon - na
out - ta here. __ Drink all night __ and talk - ing shit all day, __ I'm gon - na

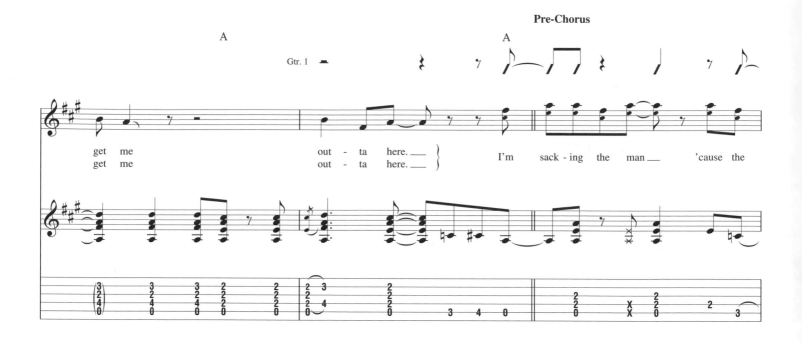

get me out - ta here. ___ I'm sack - ing the man ___ 'cause the
get me out - ta here. ___

man is a thief. ___ I'm

(cont in notation)

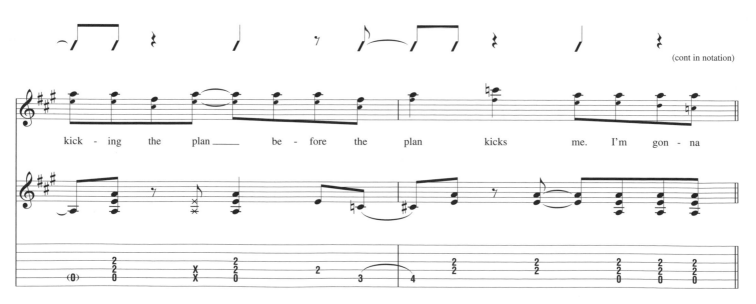

kick - ing the plan ___ be - fore the plan kicks me. I'm gon - na

Chorus

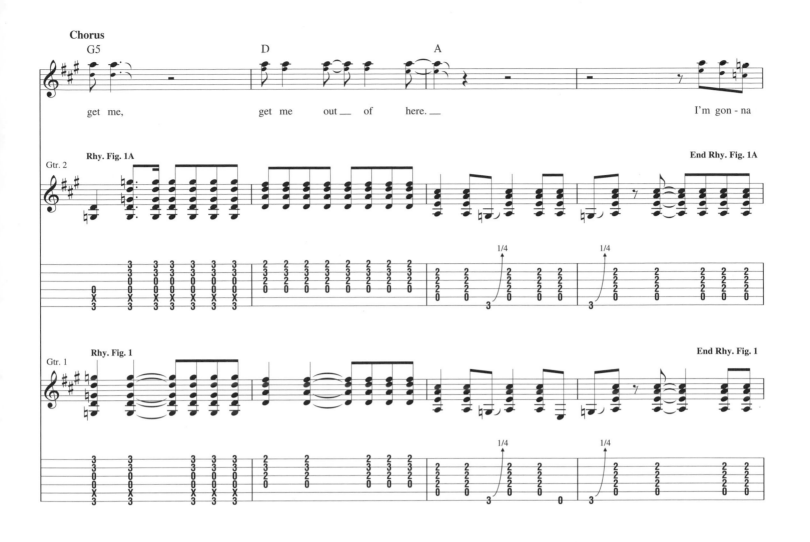

get me,   get me out __ of here. __   I'm gon-na

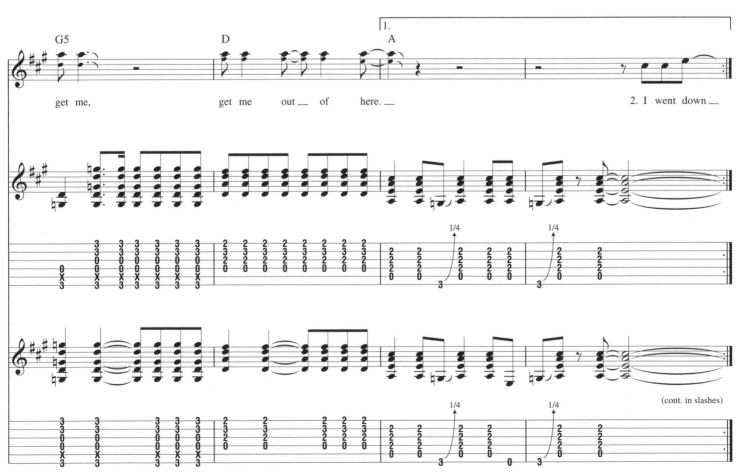

get me,   get me out __ of here. __   2. I went down __

(cont. in slashes)

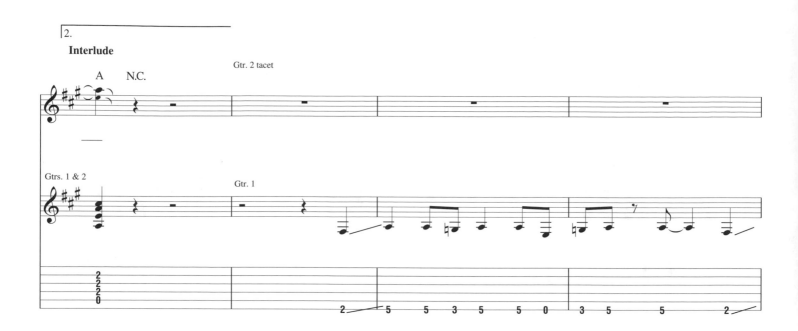

Interlude

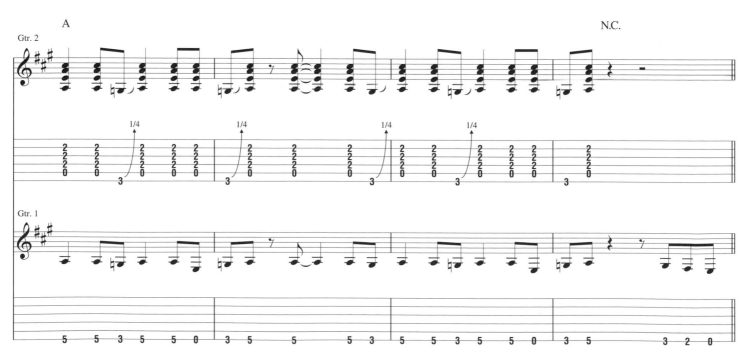

Bridge

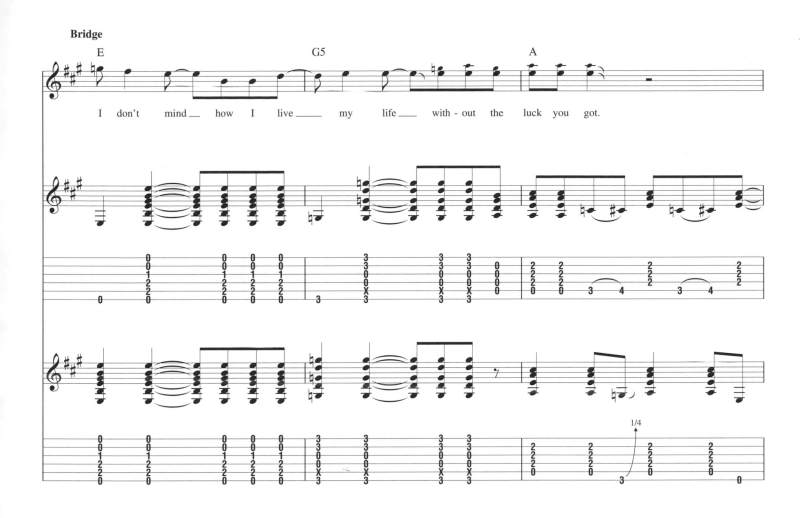

I don't mind__ how I live__ my life__ with - out the luck you got.

But I ain't try'n'__ to keep in time,__ so just keep

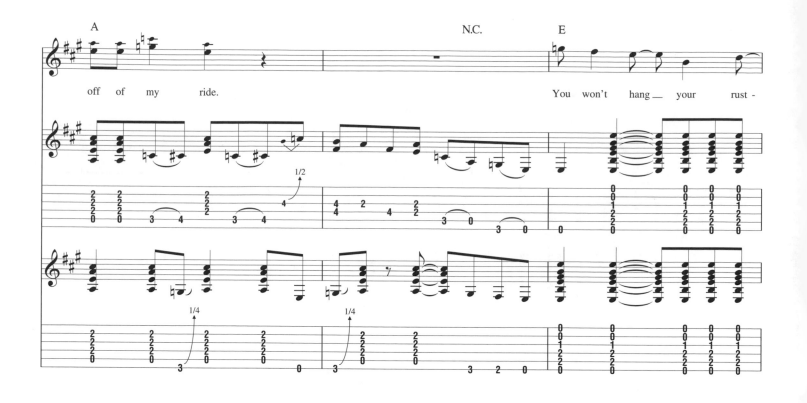

off of my ride.　　　　You won't hang＿ your rust-

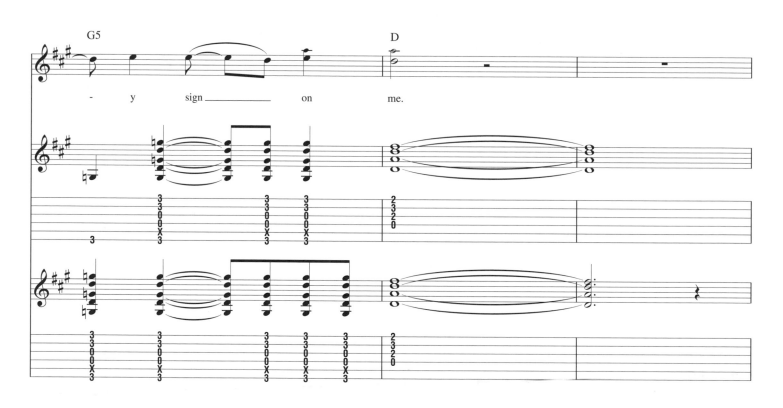

-y sign ＿＿＿ on me.

Gtr. 2 tacet

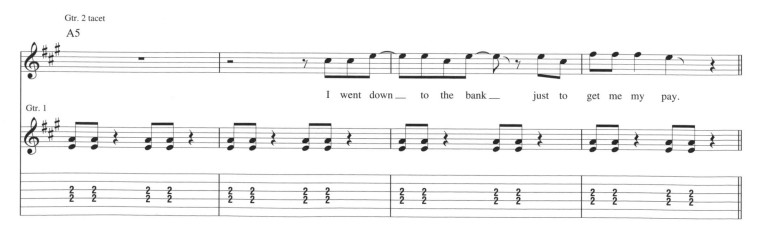

I went down＿ to the bank＿ just to get me my pay.

Gtr. 1

Chorus
Gtrs. 1 & 2: w/ Rhy. Figs. 1 & 1A (3 3/4 times)

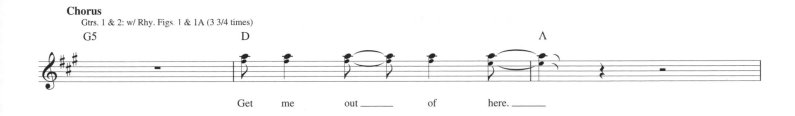

Get me out _____ of here. _____

I'm gon - na get me, get me out _____ of here, _____

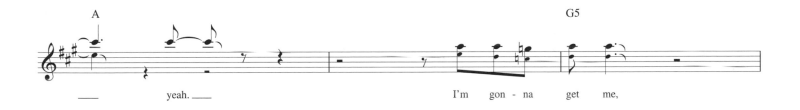

_____ yeah. _____ I'm gon - na get me,

get me out _____ of here. _____ I'm gon - na

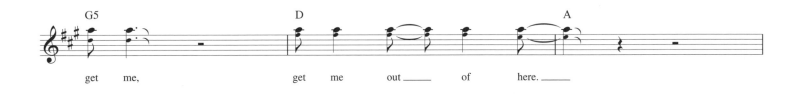

get me, get me out _____ of here. _____

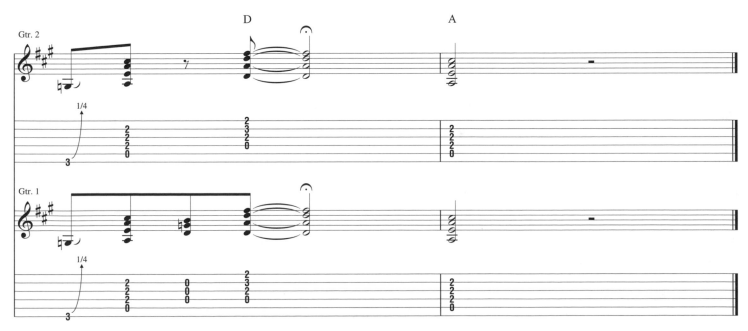

Cold Hard Bitch

Words and Music by Nic Cester, Chris Cester and Cameron Muncey

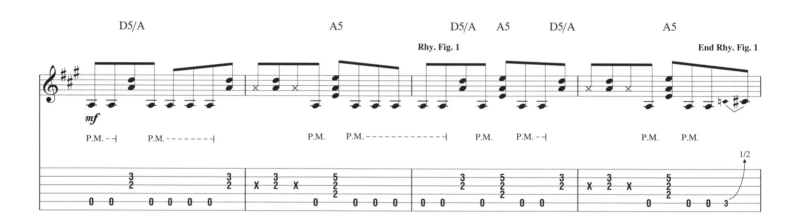

*Chord symbols refer to Gtr. 2 only.

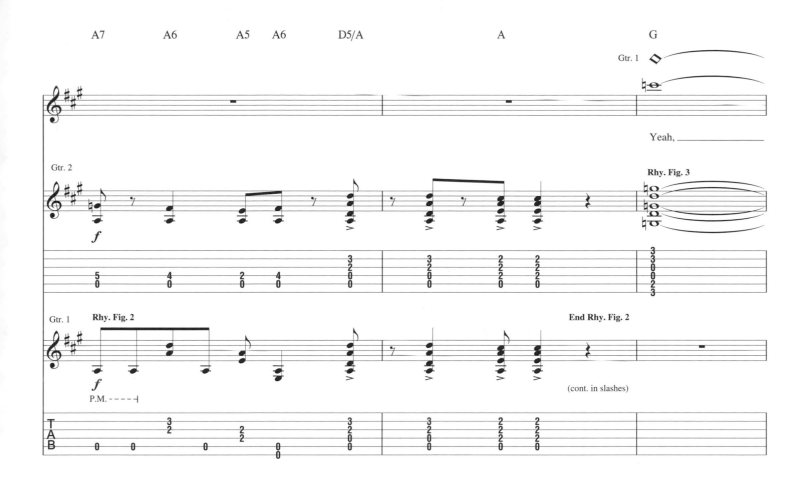

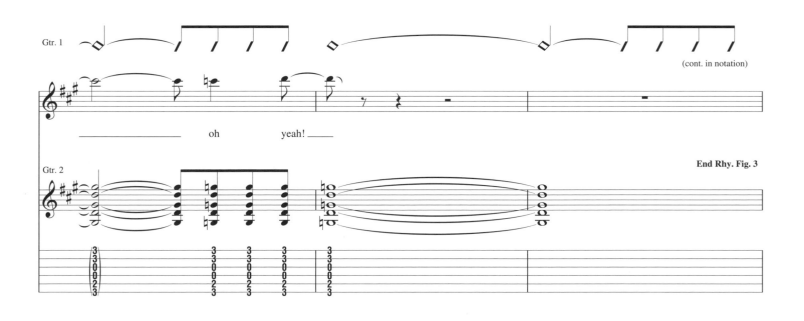

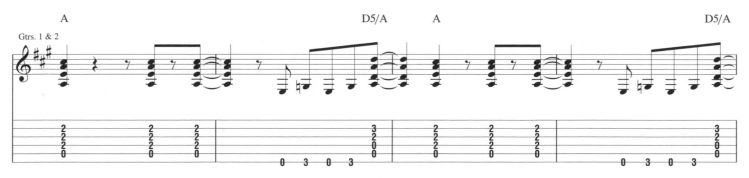

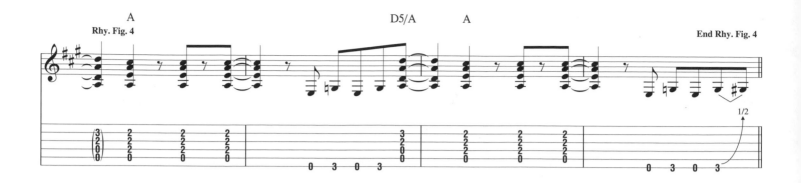

§ **Verse**

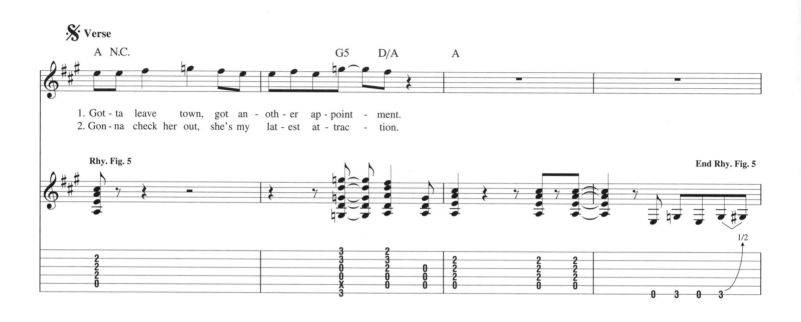

1. Got - ta leave town, got an - oth - er ap - point - ment.
2. Gon - na check her out, she's my lat - est at - trac - tion.

Gtrs. 1 & 2: w/ Rhy. Fig. 5

Spent all my rent, girl, you know I en - joyed __ it, yeah! __
Gon - na hang a - round, wan - na get a re - ac - tion, yeah! _____

Ain't

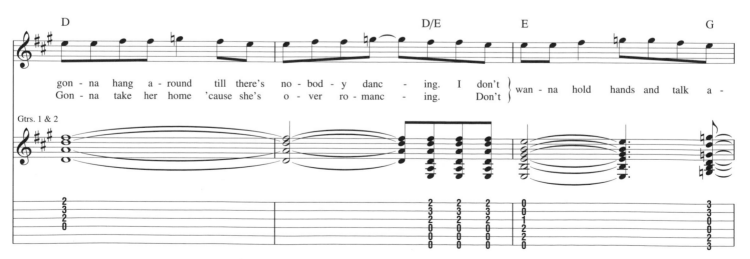

gon - na hang a - round till there's no - bod - y danc - ing. I don't } wan - na hold hands and talk a -
Gon - na take her home 'cause she's o - ver ro - manc - ing. Don't }

D.S. al Coda

Gtrs. 1 & 2: w/ Rhy. Fig. 4

⊕ Coda

Cold hard bitch, __ she was shak-in' her hips, __ well, that was all that I need. __ I'm

wait-ing, give me. Cold hard bitch. __ Just a kiss on the lips __ and I was on my knees. __

Bridge

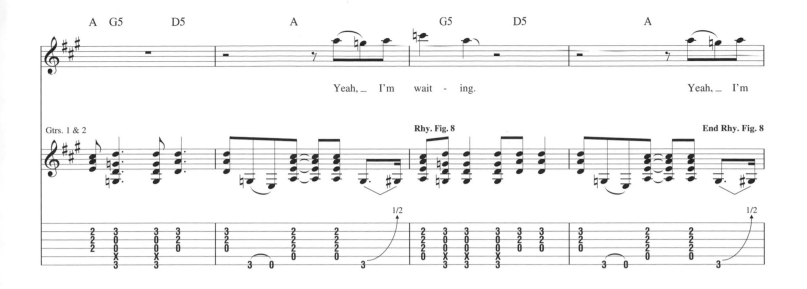

Yeah, __ I'm wait - ing.   Yeah, __ I'm

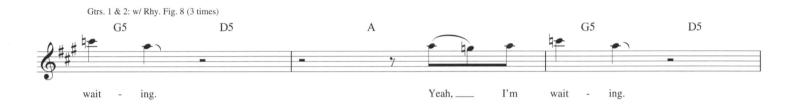

wait - ing.   Yeah, ___ I'm wait - ing.

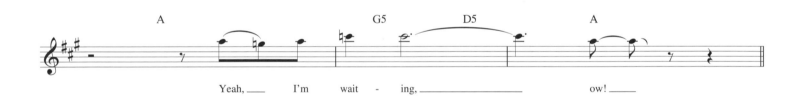

Yeah, ___ I'm wait - ing, _____ ow! ___

Interlude

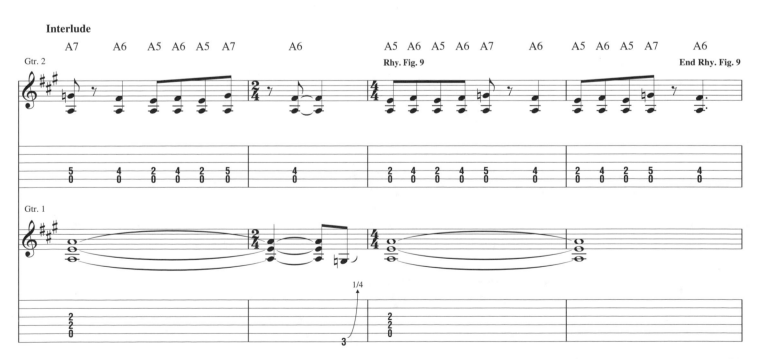

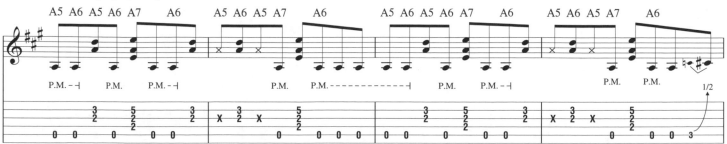

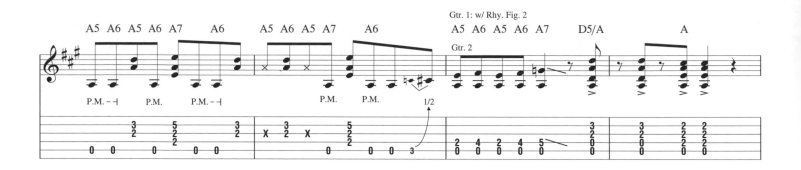

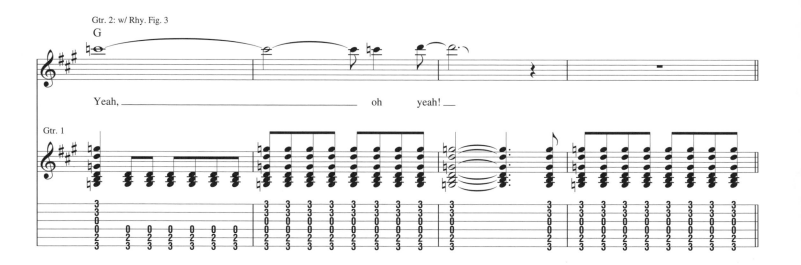

Chorus

Gtrs. 1 & 2: w/ Rhy. Fig. 6 (3 times)

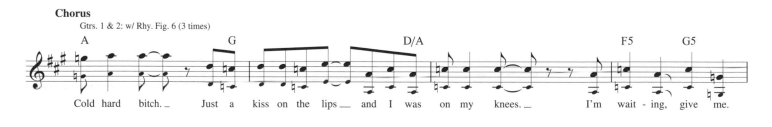

Cold hard bitch.__ Just a kiss on the lips__ and I was on my knees.__ I'm wait-ing, give me.

Cold hard bitch,__ she was shak-in' her hips,__ well, that was all that I need.__ I'm wait-ing, give me.

Cold hard bitch.__ Just a kiss on the lips__ and I was on my knees.__ I'm wait-ing, give me.

Come Around Again

Words and Music by Nic Cester and Cameron Muncey

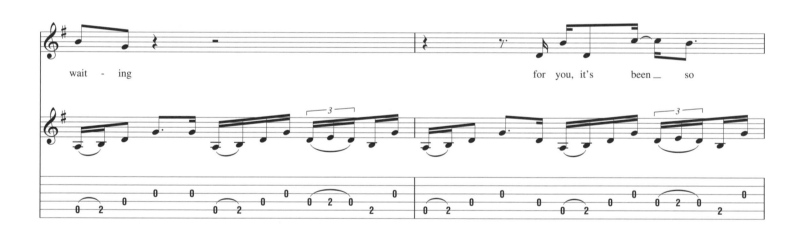

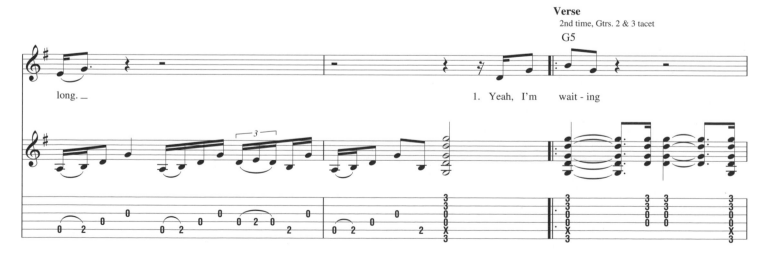

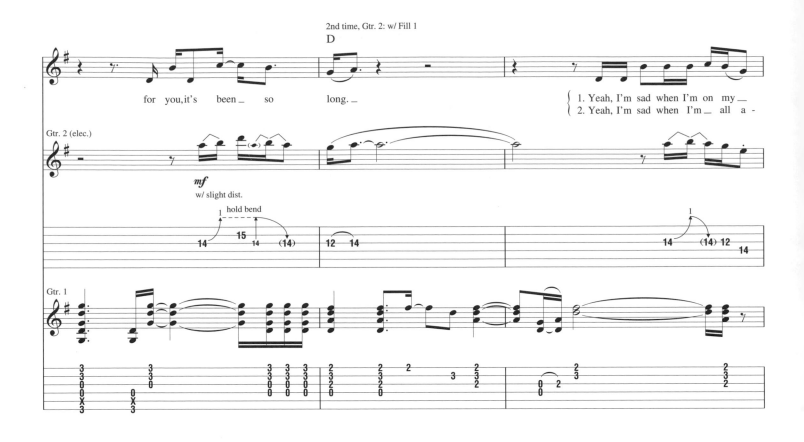

2nd time, Gtr. 2: w/ Fill 1

for you, it's been so long.

1. Yeah, I'm sad when I'm on my
2. Yeah, I'm sad when I'm all a-

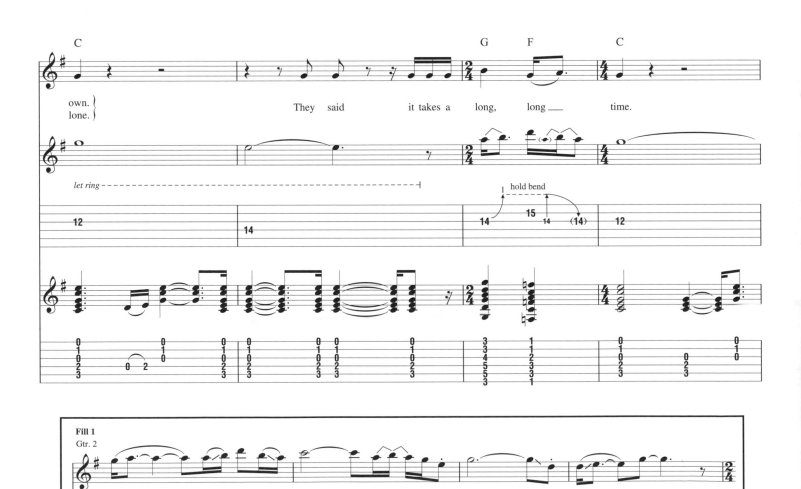

own.
lone.

They said it takes a long, long time.

Fill 1
Gtr. 2

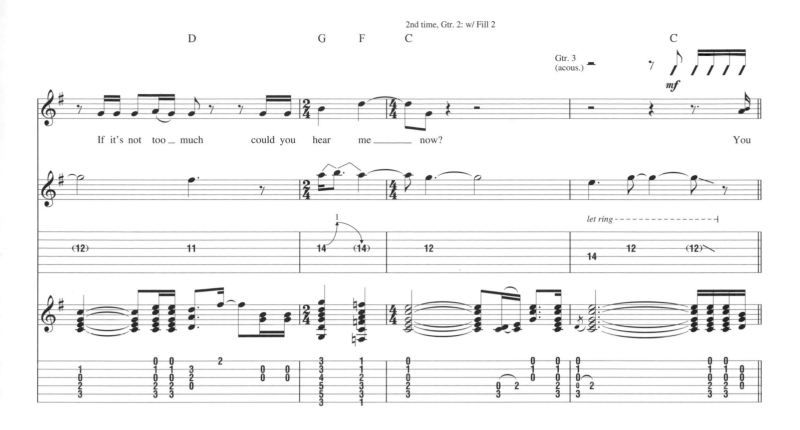

2nd time, Gtr. 2: w/ Fill 2

If it's not too __ much could you hear me _____ now? You

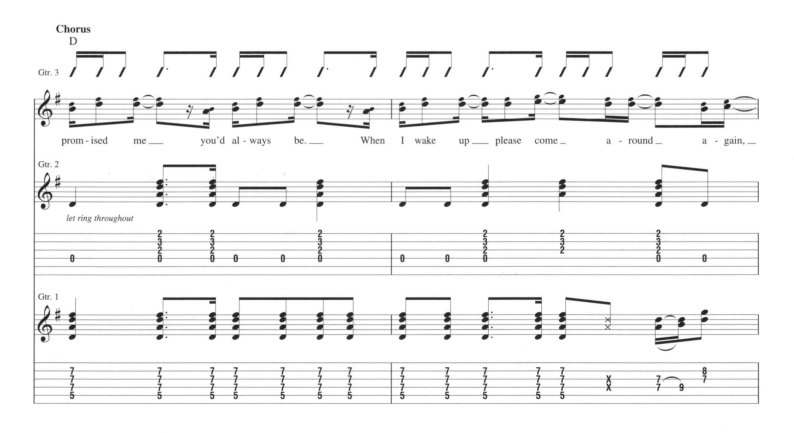

Chorus

prom-ised me __ you'd al-ways be. __ When I wake up __ please come __ a-round __ a-gain, __

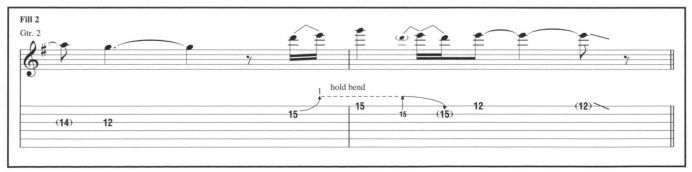

Fill 2

come a-round a-gain. ____ You

prom-ised me ____ you'd al-ways be. ____ When I wake up ____ please come ____ a-round ____ a-gain,

come a-round a-gain. ___ Yeah. ___

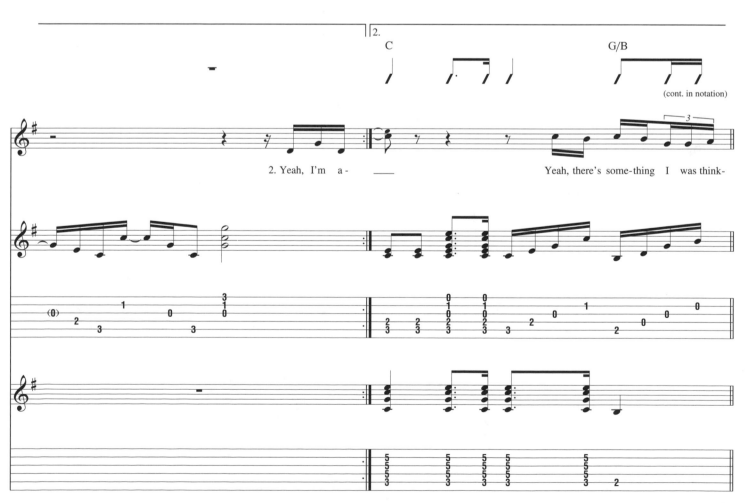

2. Yeah, I'm a- ___   Yeah, there's some-thing I was think-

(cont. in notation)

Bridge

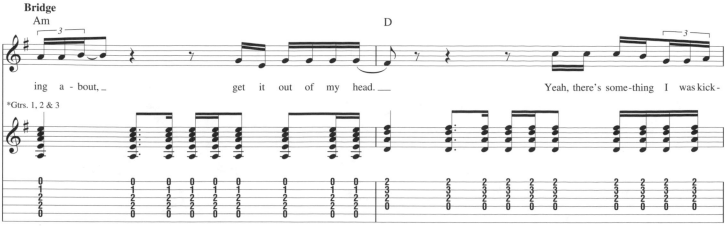

*Composite arrangement

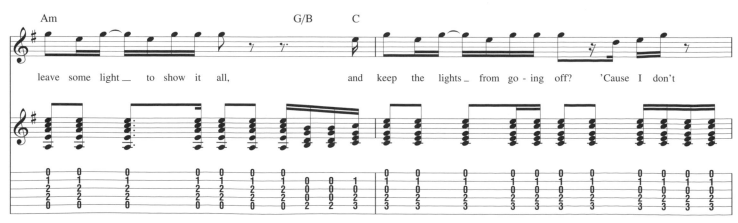

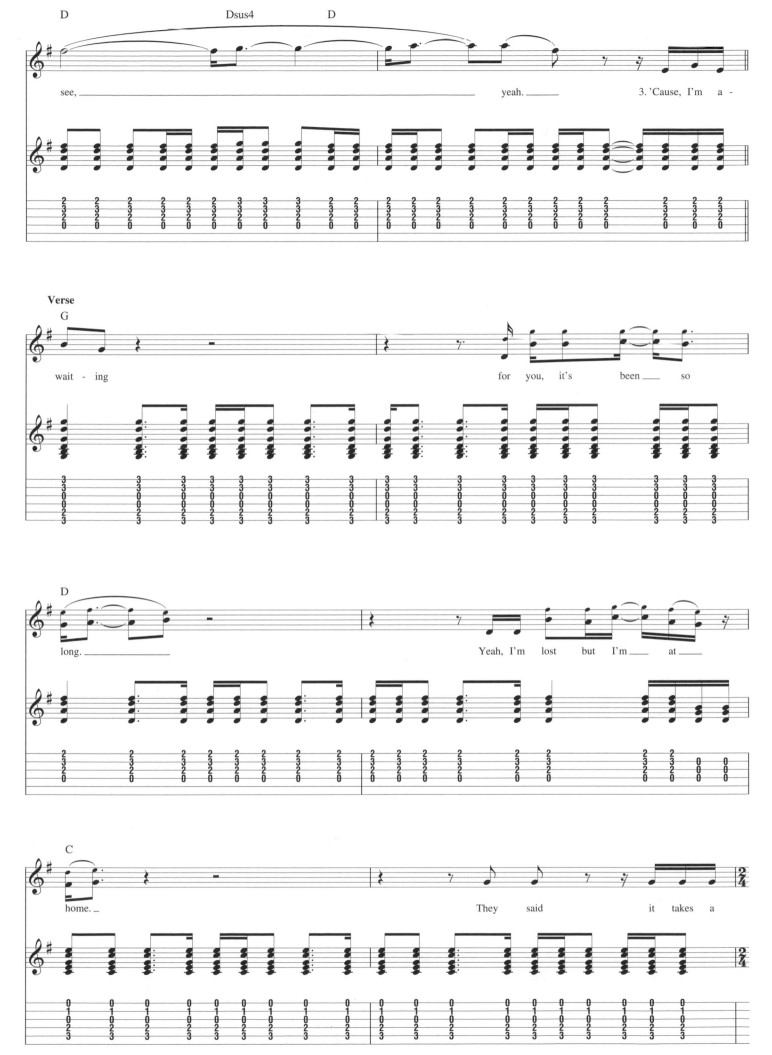

Take It or Leave It

Words and Music by Nic Cester, Chris Cester and Cameron Muncey

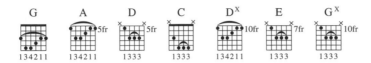

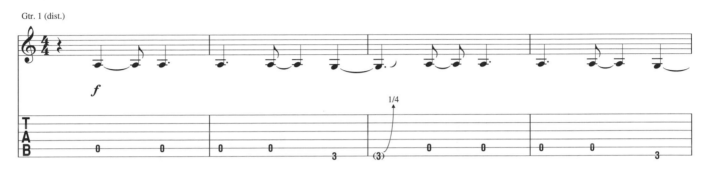

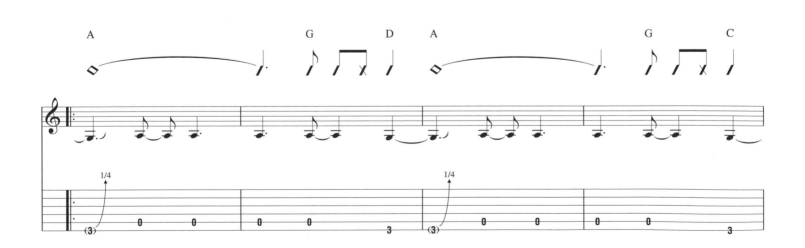

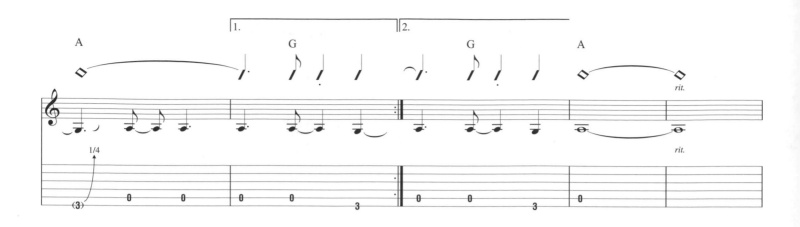

Slower ♩ = 172

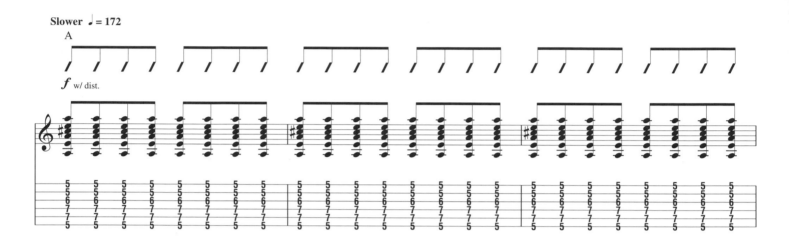

Verse
2nd time, Gtr. 1: w/ Rhy. Fill 1

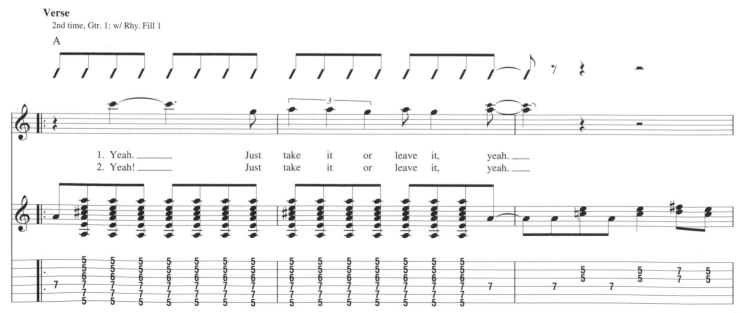

1. Yeah._____ Just take it or leave it, yeah._____
2. Yeah!_____ Just take it or leave it, yeah._____

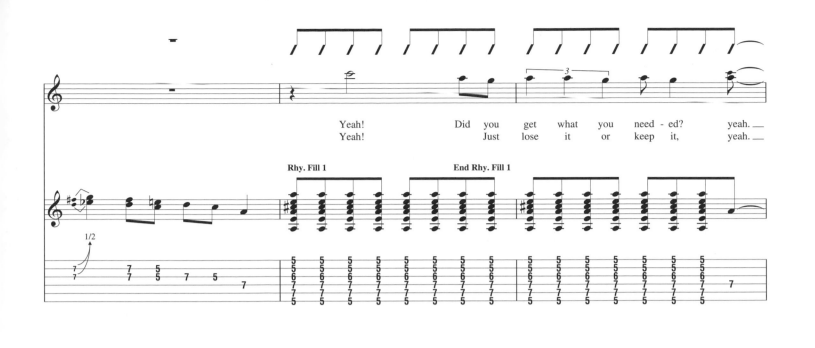

Yeah! Did you get what you need - ed? yeah.___
Yeah! Just lose it or keep it, yeah.___

Rhy. Fill 1   End Rhy. Fill 1

Come on,___ don't you___
Come on, I think you___

___ know what you got to do?___ ___
___ know what you've got to do.___

A

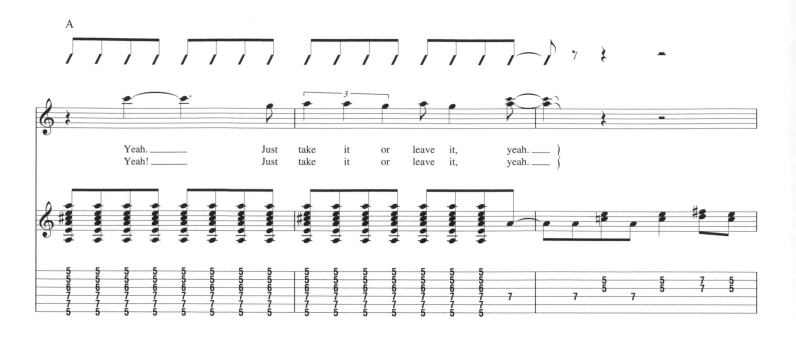

Yeah. _____ Just take it or leave it, yeah. _____
Yeah! _____ Just take it or leave it, yeah. _____

E   **G**ˣ

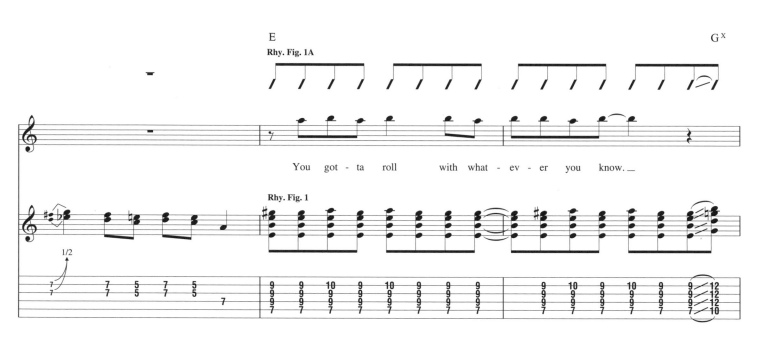

Rhy. Fig. 1A

You got - ta roll   with what - ev - er   you know. __

Rhy. Fig. 1

N.C.

End Rhy. Fig. 1A

(cont. in notation)

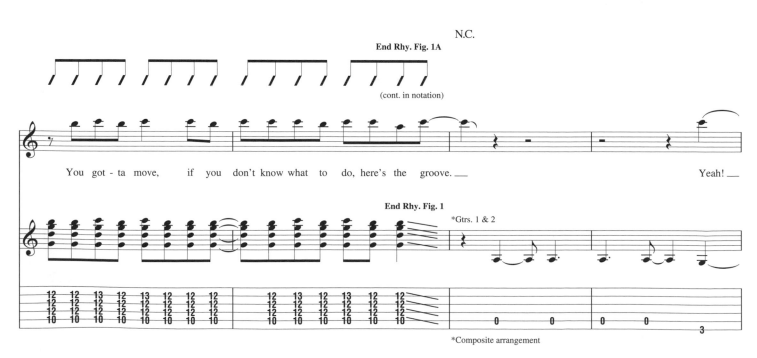

You got - ta move,   if you don't know what to   do, here's the   groove. __   Yeah! __

End Rhy. Fig. 1

*Gtrs. 1 & 2

*Composite arrangement

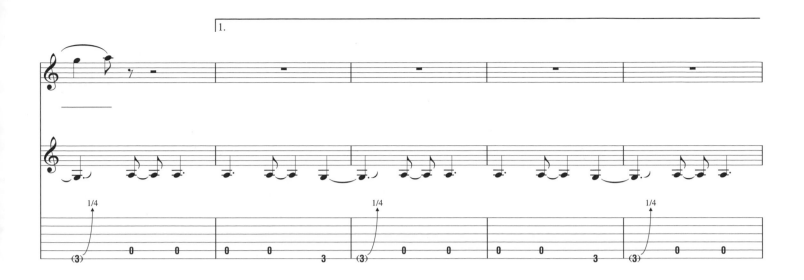

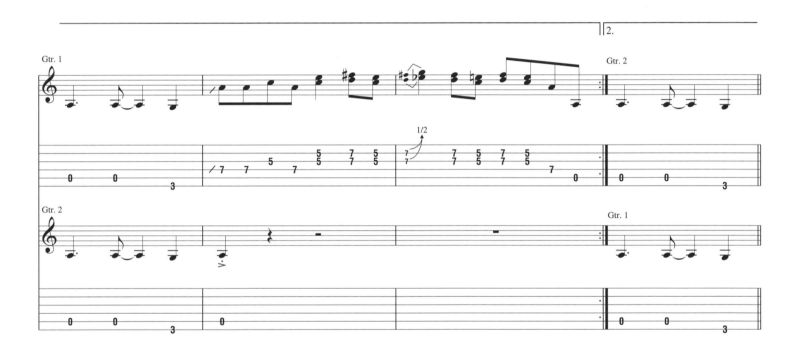

Interlude

N.C.

Guitar Solo

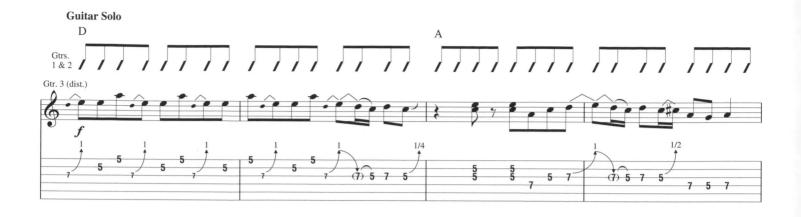

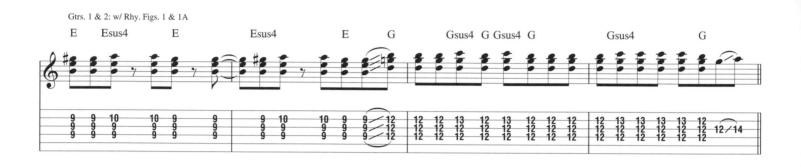

Outro

Yeah! __ Just take it or leave it, yeah. __ I said now, take it or leave it, yeah. __

__ I said, just take it or leave it, yeah. __ I said, just take it or leave it!

Lazy Gun

Words and Music by Nic Cester and Chris Cester

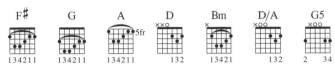

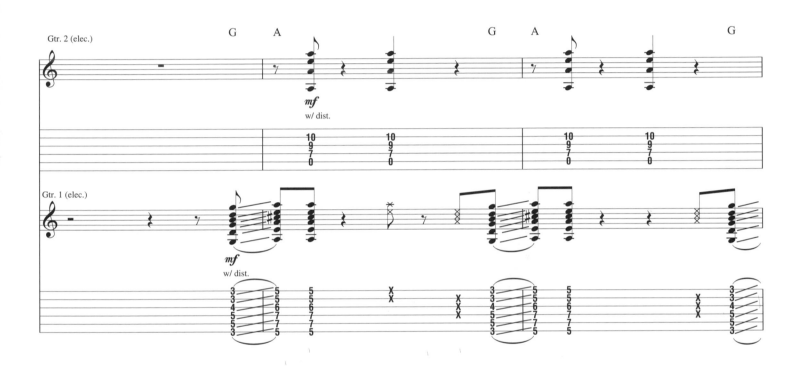

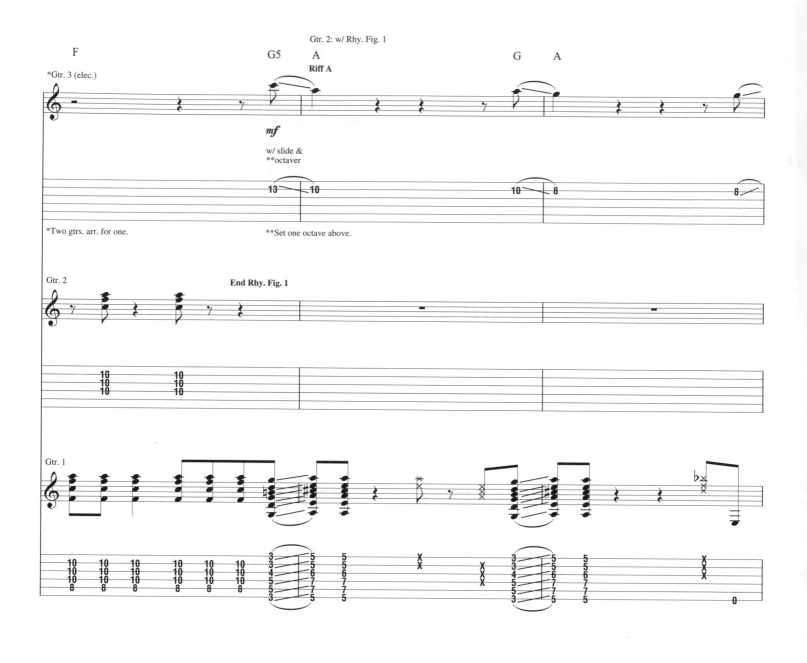

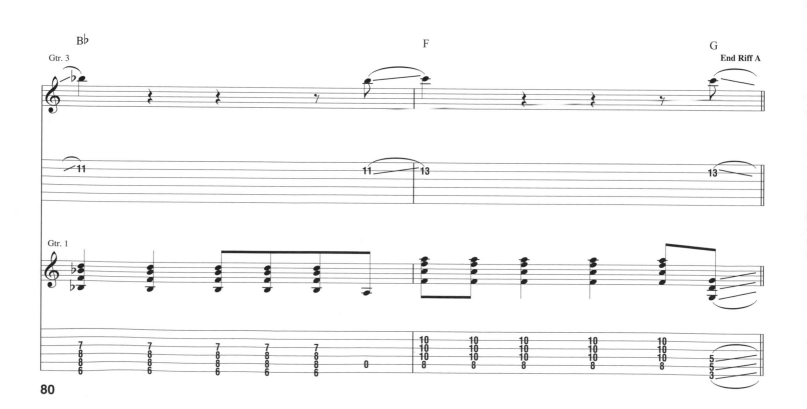

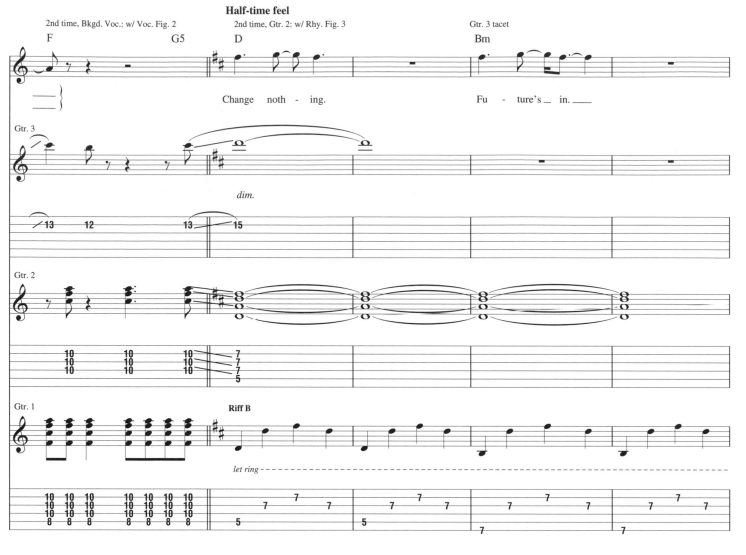

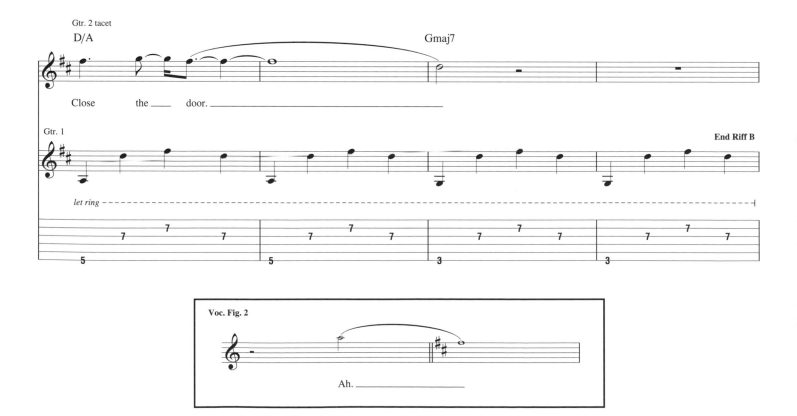

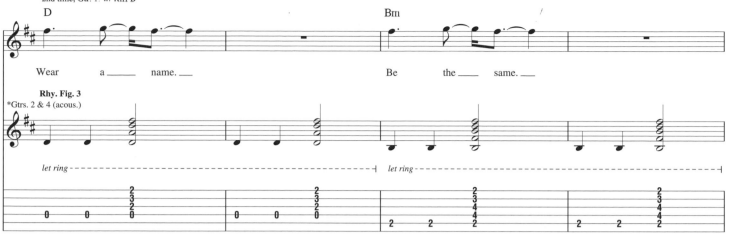

Wear a ___ name. ___ Be the ___ same. ___

*Composite arrangement

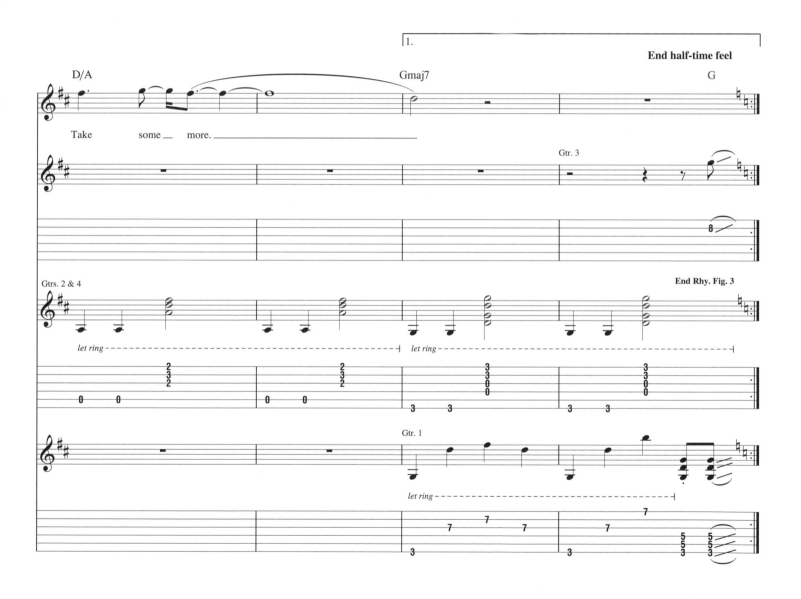

Take some __ more. ____

Change noth - ing. ___ The fu - ture's in. ___

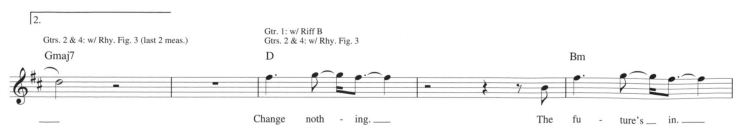

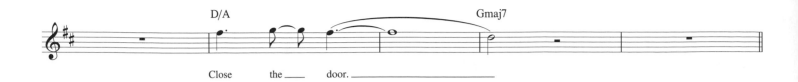

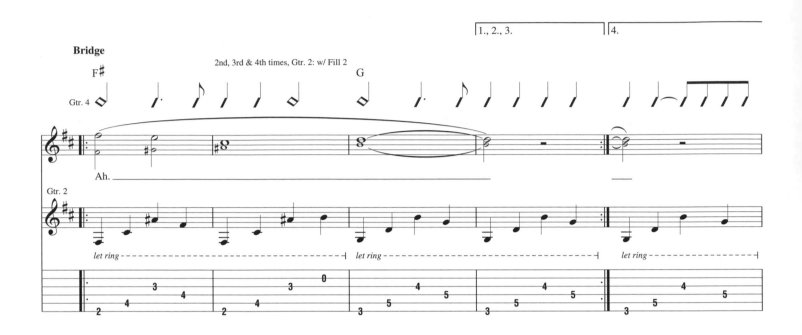

Close the ___ door. ___

Bridge

2nd, 3rd & 4th times, Gtr. 2: w/ Fill 2

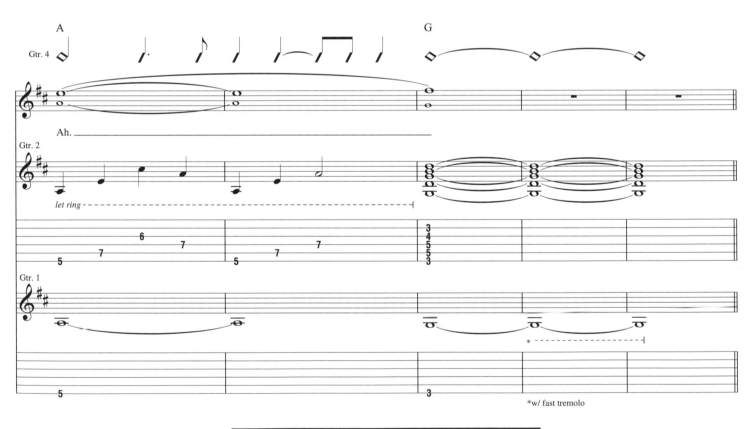

Ah. ___

*w/ fast tremolo

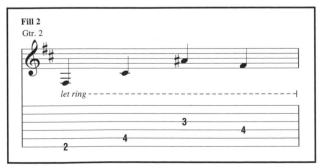

Chorus

Change noth- ing. ____ The fu- ture's_ in. ____

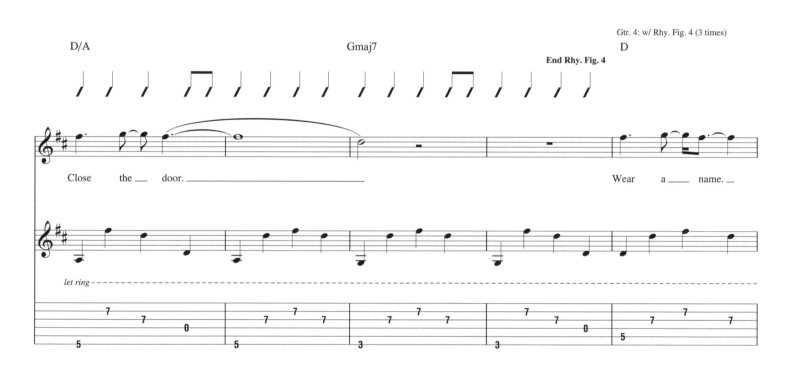

Close the __ door. _____ Wear a __ name. __

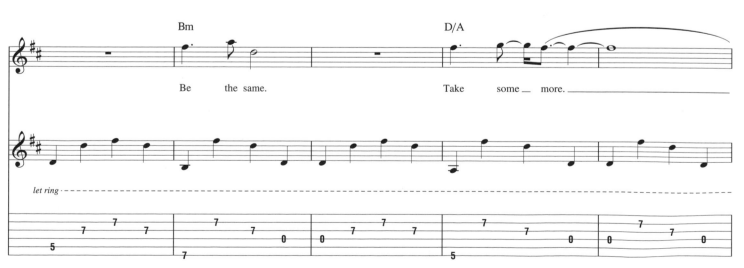

Be the same. Take some_ more. _____

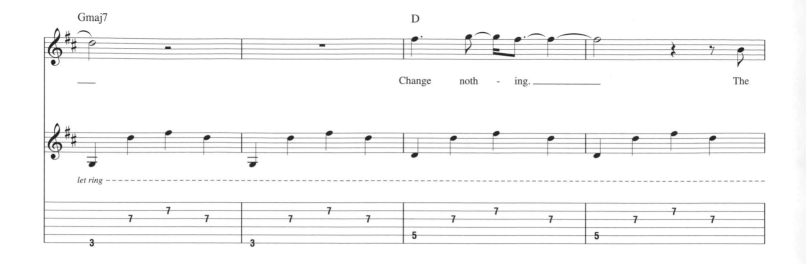

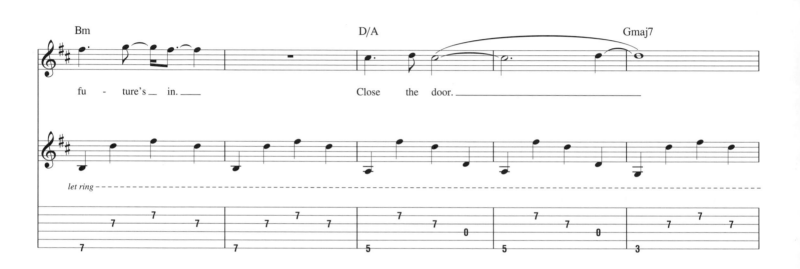

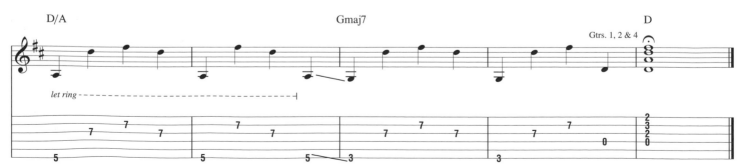

Timothy

Words and Music by Chris Cester

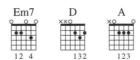

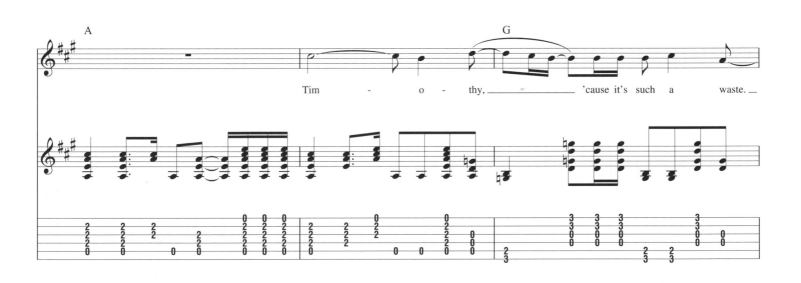

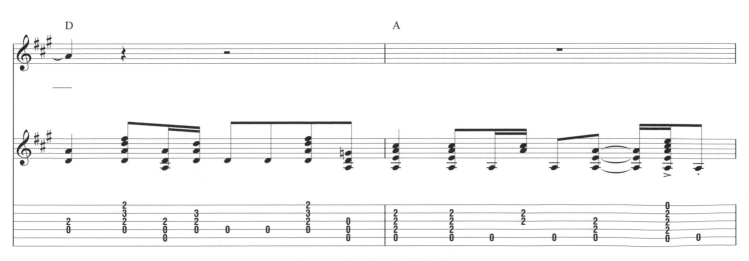

Tim - o - thy, ____ we found ____ your space - ship. Tim - o - thy, it's the far-

- thest you've _ ev - er flown. ____ Nev - er used _

your head _____ to find out what ___ this whole ___ thing meant.

End Rhy. Fig. 1

(cont. in slashes)

Chorus

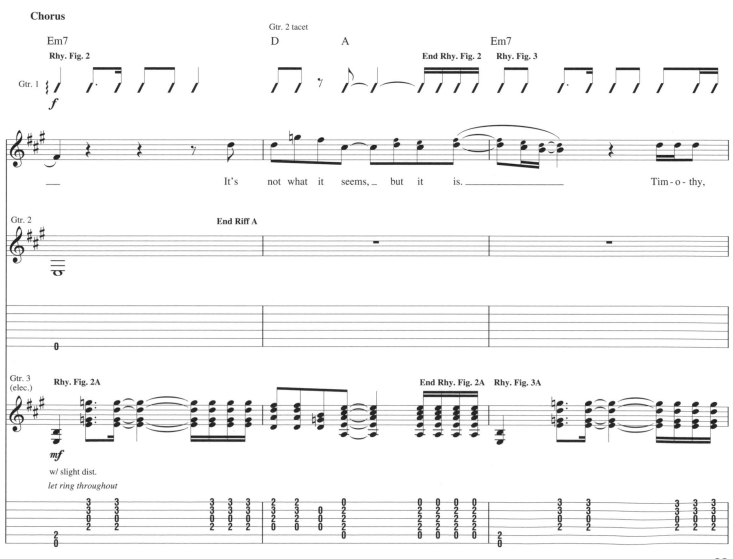

Em7

Rhy. Fig. 2

Gtr. 1

f

Gtr. 2 tacet

D   A   Em7

End Rhy. Fig. 2   **Rhy. Fig. 3**

___ It's not what it seems, __ but it is. _____ Tim - o - thy,

Gtr. 2

End Riff A

Gtr. 3
(elec.)   **Rhy. Fig. 2A**

mf

w/ slight dist.

let ring throughout

End Rhy. Fig. 2A   **Rhy. Fig. 3A**

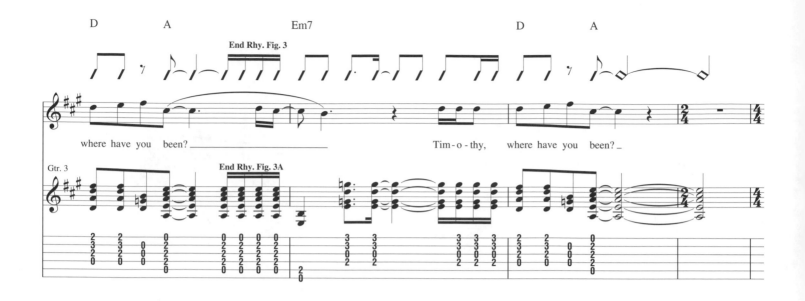

where have you been? _____ Tim-o-thy, where have you been? _

2. Tim - o - thy, ____ where did you go? ___

Tim - o - thy, _____ the boy can throw. ___

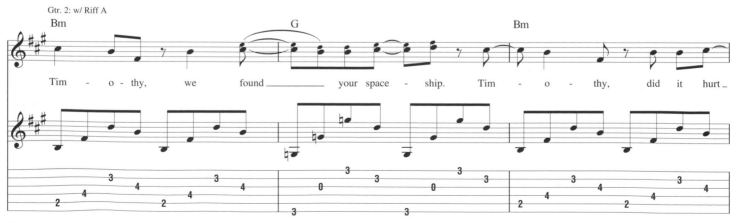

Tim - o - thy, we found _____ your space - ship. Tim - o - thy, did it hurt _

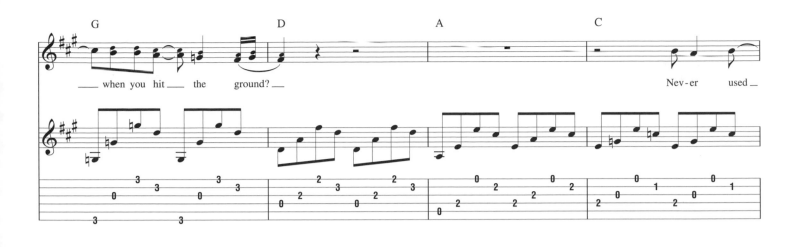

when you hit the ground? Nev-er used

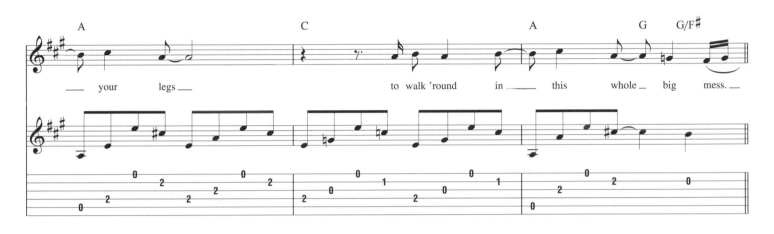

your legs to walk 'round in this whole big mess.

Chorus

Gtrs. 1 & 3: w/ Rhy. Figs. 2 & 2A

Gtrs. 1 & 3: w/ Rhy. Figs. 3 & 3A (2 times)

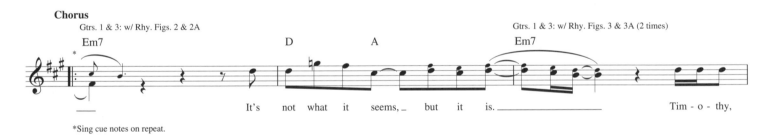

It's not what it seems, but it is. Tim-o-thy,

*Sing cue notes on repeat.

where have you been? She cried in the kit-chen to let

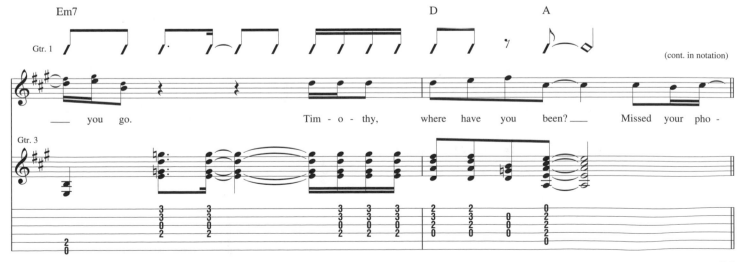

you go. Tim-o-thy, where have you been? Missed your pho-

Bridge

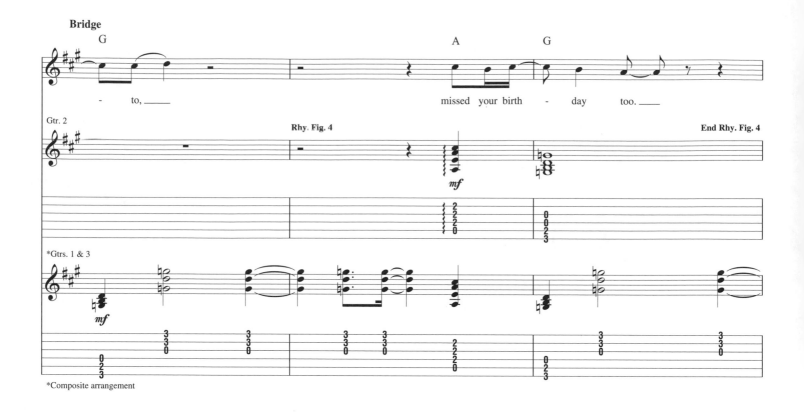

*Composite arrangement

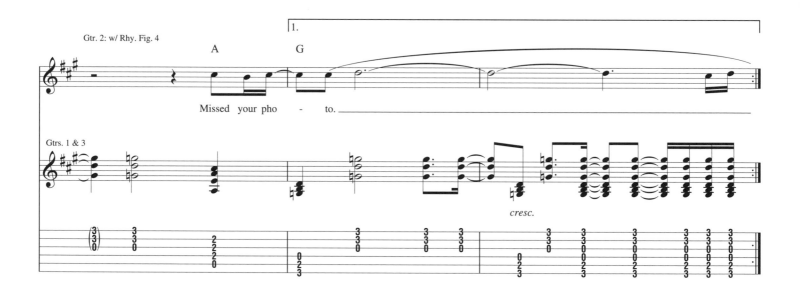

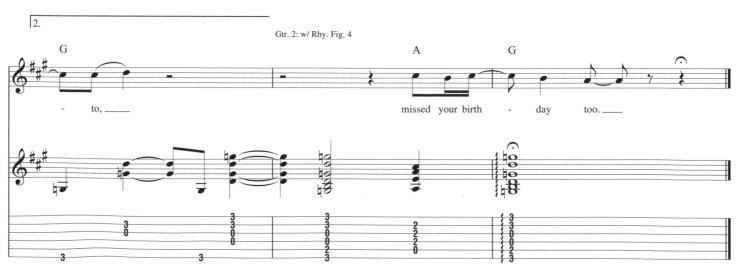

Guitar Notation Legend

Guitar Music can be notated three different ways: on a *musical staff*, in *tablature*, and in *rhythm slashes*.

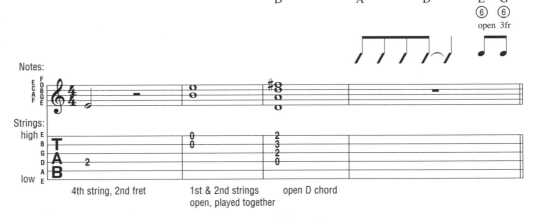

RHYTHM SLASHES are written above the staff. Strum chords in the rhythm indicated. Use the chord diagrams found at the top of the first page of the transcription for the appropriate chord voicings. Round noteheads indicate single notes.

THE MUSICAL STAFF shows pitches and rhythms and is divided by bar lines into measures. Pitches are named after the first seven letters of the alphabet.

TABLATURE graphically represents the guitar fingerboard. Each horizontal line represents a a string, and each number represents a fret.

4th string, 2nd fret   1st & 2nd strings open, played together   open D chord

Definitions for Special Guitar Notation

HALF-STEP BEND: Strike the note and bend up 1/2 step.

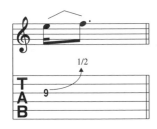

WHOLE-STEP BEND: Strike the note and bend up one step.

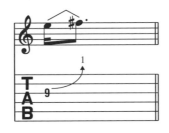

GRACE NOTE BEND: Strike the note and immediately bend up as indicated.

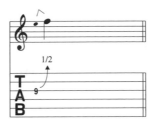

SLIGHT (MICROTONE) BEND: Strike the note and bend up 1/4 step.

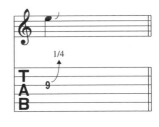

BEND AND RELEASE: Strike the note and bend up as indicated, then release back to the original note. Only the first note is struck.

PRE-BEND: Bend the note as indicated, then strike it.

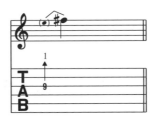

PRE-BEND AND RELEASE: Bend the note as indicated. Strike it and release the bend back to the original note.

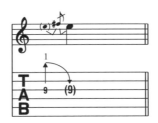

UNISON BEND: Strike the two notes simultaneously and bend the lower note up to the pitch of the higher.

VIBRATO: The string is vibrated by rapidly bending and releasing the note with the fretting hand.

WIDE VIBRATO: The pitch is varied to a greater degree by vibrating with the fretting hand.

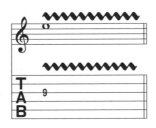

HAMMER-ON: Strike the first (lower) note with one finger, then sound the higher note (on the same string) with another finger by fretting it without picking.

PULL-OFF: Place both fingers on the notes to be sounded. Strike the first note and without picking, pull the finger off to sound the second (lower) note.

LEGATO SLIDE: Strike the first note and then slide the same fret-hand finger up or down to the second note. The second note is not struck.

SHIFT SLIDE: Same as legato slide, except the second note is struck.

TRILL: Very rapidly alternate between the notes indicated by continuously hammering on and pulling off.

TAPPING: Hammer ("tap") the fret indicated with the pick-hand index or middle finger and pull off to the note fretted by the fret hand.

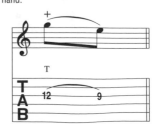

NATURAL HARMONIC: Strike the note while the fret-hand lightly touches the string directly over the fret indicated.

PINCH HARMONIC: The note is fretted normally and a harmonic is produced by adding the edge of the thumb or the tip of the index finger of the pick hand to the normal pick attack.

HARP HARMONIC: The note is fretted normally and a harmonic is produced by gently resting the pick hand's index finger directly above the indicated fret (in parentheses) while the pick hand's thumb or pick assists by plucking the appropriate string.

PICK SCRAPE: The edge of the pick is rubbed down (or up) the string, producing a scratchy sound.

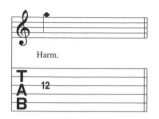

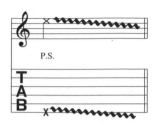

MUFFLED STRINGS: A percussive sound is produced by laying the fret hand across the string(s) without depressing, and striking them with the pick hand.

PALM MUTING: The note is partially muted by the pick hand lightly touching the string(s) just before the bridge.

RAKE: Drag the pick across the strings indicated with a single motion.

TREMOLO PICKING: The note is picked as rapidly and continuously as possible.

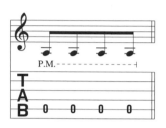

ARPEGGIATE: Play the notes of the chord indicated by quickly rolling them from bottom to top.

VIBRATO BAR DIVE AND RETURN: The pitch of the note or chord is dropped a specified number of steps (in rhythm) then returned to the original pitch.

VIBRATO BAR SCOOP: Depress the bar just before striking the note, then quickly release the bar.

VIBRATO BAR DIP: Strike the note and then immediately drop a specified number of steps, then release back to the original pitch.

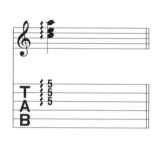

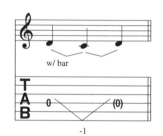

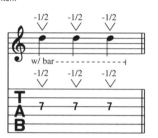

Additional Musical Definitions

(accent)	• Accentuate note (play it louder)	
(accent)	• Accentuate note with great intensity	
(staccato)	• Play the note short	
⊓	• Downstroke	
∨	• Upstroke	

Rhy. Fig. • Label used to recall a recurring accompaniment pattern (usually chordal).

Riff • Label used to recall composed, melodic lines (usually single notes) which recur.

Fill • Label used to identify a brief melodic figure which is to be inserted into the arrangement.

Rhy. Fill • A chordal version of a Fill.

tacet • Instrument is silent (drops out).

D.S. al Coda • Go back to the sign (𝄋), then play until the measure marked "**To Coda**," then skip to the section labelled "**Coda**."

D.C. al Fine • Go back to the beginning of the song and play until the measure marked "*Fine*" (end).

• Repeat measures between signs.

• When a repeated section has different endings, play the first ending only the first time and the second ending only the second time.

NOTE: Tablature numbers in parentheses mean:
1. The note is being sustained over a system (note in standard notation is tied), or
2. The note is sustained, but a new articulation (such as a hammer-on, pull-off, slide or vibrato begins), or
3. The note is a barely audible "ghost" note (note in standard notation is also in parentheses).

RECORDED VERSIONS

The Best Note-For-Note Transcriptions Available

ALL BOOKS INCLUDE TABLATURE

GUITAR PLAY-ALONG

This series will help you play your favorite songs quickly and easily. Just follow the tab and listen to the CD to hear how the guitar should sound, and then play along using the separate backing tracks. Mac or PC users can also slow down the tempo by using the CD in their computer. The melody and lyrics are also included in the book so that you can sing or simply follow along.

VOL. 1 – ROCK GUITAR   00699570 / $12.95
Day Tripper • Message in a Bottle • Refugee • Shattered • Sunshine of Your Love • Takin' Care of Business • Tush • Walk This Way.

VOL. 2 – ACOUSTIC   00699569 / $12.95
Angie • Behind Blue Eyes • Best of My Love • Blackbird • Dust in the Wind • Layla • Night Moves • Yesterday.

VOL. 3 – HARD ROCK   00699573 / $14.95
Crazy Train • Iron Man • Living After Midnight • Rock You Like a Hurricane • Round and Round • Smoke on the Water • Sweet Child O' Mine • You Really Got Me.

VOL. 4 – POP/ROCK   00699571 / $12.95
Breakdown • Crazy Little Thing Called Love • Hit Me with Your Best Shot • I Want You to Want Me • Lights • R.O.C.K. in the U.S.A. (A Salute to 60's Rock) • Summer of '69 • What I Like About You.

VOL. 5 – MODERN ROCK   00699574 / $12.95
Aerials • Alive • Bother • Chop Suey! • Control • Last Resort • Take a Look Around (Theme from "M:I-2") • Wish You Were Here.

VOL. 6 – '90S ROCK   00699572 / $12.95
Are You Gonna Go My Way • Come Out and Play • I'll Stick Around • Know Your Enemy • Man in the Box • Outshined • Smells Like Teen Spirit • Under the Bridge.

VOL. 7 – BLUES GUITAR   00699575 / $12.95
All Your Love (I Miss Loving) • Born Under a Bad Sign • Hide Away • I'm Tore Down • I'm Your Hoochie Coochie Man • Pride and Joy • Sweet Home Chicago • The Thrill Is Gone.

VOL. 8 – ROCK   00699585 / $12.95
All Right Now • Black Magic Woman • Get Back • Hey Joe • Layla • Love Me Two Times • Won't Get Fooled Again • You Really Got Me.

VOL. 9 – PUNK ROCK   00699576 / $12.95
All the Small Things • Fat Lip • Flavor of the Weak • I Feel So • Lifestyles of the Rich and Famous • (So) Tired of Waiting for You • Say It Ain't So • Self Esteem.

VOL. 10 – ACOUSTIC   00699586 / $12.95
Here Comes the Sun • Landslide • The Magic Bus • Norwegian Wood (This Bird Has Flown) • Pink Houses • Space Oddity • Tangled Up in Blue • Tears in Heaven.

VOL. 11 – EARLY ROCK   00699579 / $12.95
Fun, Fun, Fun • Hound Dog • Louie, Louie • No Particular Place to Go • Oh, Pretty Woman • Rock Around the Clock • Under the Boardwalk • Wild Thing.

VOL. 12 – POP/ROCK   00699587 / $12.95
867-5309/Jenny • Every Breath You Take • Money for Nothing • Rebel, Rebel • Run to You • Ticket to Ride • Wonderful Tonight • You Give Love a Bad Name.

VOL. 13 – FOLK ROCK   00699581 / $12.95
Annie's Song • Leaving on a Jet Plane • Suite: Judy Blue Eyes • This Land Is Your Land • Time in a Bottle • Turn! Turn! Turn! (To Everything There Is a Season) • You've Got a Friend • You've Got to Hide Your Love Away.

VOL. 14 – BLUES ROCK   00699582 / $14.95
Blue on Black • Crossfire • Cross Road Blues (Crossroads) • The House Is Rockin' • La Grange • Move It on Over • Roadhouse Blues • Statesboro Blues.

VOL. 15 – R&B   00699583 / $12.95
Ain't Too Proud to Beg • Brick House • Get Ready • I Can't Help Myself (Sugar Pie, Honey Bunch) • I Got You (I Feel Good) • I Heard It Through the Grapevine • My Girl • Shining Star.

VOL. 16 – JAZZ   00699584 / $12.95
All Blues • Bluesette • Footprints • How Insensitive (Insensatez) • Misty • Satin Doll • Stella by Starlight • Tenor Madness.

VOL. 17 – COUNTRY   00699588 / $12.95
Amie • Boot Scootin' Boogie • Chattahoochee • Folsom Prison Blues • Friends in Low Places • Forever and Ever, Amen • T-R-O-U-B-L-E • Workin' Man Blues.

VOL. 18 – ACOUSTIC ROCK   00699577 / $14.95
About a Girl • Breaking the Girl • Drive • Iris • More Than Words • Patience • Silent Lucidity • 3 AM.

VOL. 19 – SOUL   00699578 / $12.95
Get Up (I Feel Like Being) a Sex Machine • Green Onions • In the Midnight Hour • Knock on Wood • Mustang Sally • Respect • (Sittin' On) the Dock of the Bay • Soul Man.

VOL. 20 – ROCKABILLY   00699580 / $12.95
Be-Bop-A-Lula • Blue Suede Shoes • Hello Mary Lou • Little Sister • Mystery Train • Rock This Town • Stray Cat Strut • That'll Be the Day.

VOL. 21 – YULETIDE   00699602 / $12.95
Angels We Have Heard on High • Away in a Manger • Deck the Hall • The First Noel • Go, Tell It on the Mountain • Jingle Bells • Joy to the World • O Little Town of Bethlehem.

VOL. 22 – CHRISTMAS   00699600 / $12.95
The Christmas Song (Chestnuts Roasting on an Open Fire) • Frosty the Snow Man • Happy Xmas (War Is Over) • Here Comes Santa Claus (Right Down Santa Claus Lane) • Jingle-Bell Rock • Merry Christmas, Darling • Rudolph the Red-Nosed Reindeer • Silver Bells.

VOL. 23 – SURF   00699635 / $12.95
Let's Go Trippin' • Out of Limits • Penetration • Pipeline • Surf City • Surfin' U.S.A. • Walk Don't Run • The Wedge.

VOL. 24 – ERIC CLAPTON   00699649 / $14.95
Badge • Bell Bottom Blues • Change the World • Cocaine • Key to the Highway • Lay Down Sally • White Room • Wonderful Tonight.

VOL. 25 – LENNON AND MCCARTNEY   00699642 / $14.95
Back in the U.S.S.R. • Drive My Car • Get Back • A Hard Day's Night • I Feel Fine • Paperback Writer • Revolution • Ticket to Ride.

VOL. 26 – ELVIS PRESLEY   00699643 / $14.95
All Shook Up • Blue Suede Shoes • Don't Be Cruel (To a Heart That's True) • Heartbreak Hotel • Hound Dog • Jailhouse Rock • Little Sister • Mystery Train.

VOL. 27 – DAVID LEE ROTH   00699645 / $14.95
Ain't Talkin' 'Bout Love • Dance the Night Away • Just Like Paradise • A Lil' Ain't Enough • Panama • Runnin' with the Devil • Unchained • Yankee Rose.

VOL. 28 – GREG KOCH   00699646 / $14.95
Chief's Blues • Death of a Bassman • Dylan the Villain • The Grip • Holy Grail • Spank It • Tonus Diabolicus • Zoiks.

VOL. 29 – BOB SEGER   00699647 / $14.95
Against the Wind • Betty Lou's Gettin' Out Tonight • Hollywood Nights • Mainstreet • Night Moves • Old Time Rock & Roll • Rock and Roll Never Forgets • Still the Same.

VOL. 30 – KISS   00699644 / $14.95
Cold Gin • Detroit Rock City • Deuce • Firehouse • Heaven's on Fire • Love Gun • Rock and Roll All Nite • Shock Me.

VOL. 31 – CHRISTMAS HITS   00699652 / $12.95
Blue Christmas • Do You Hear What I Hear • Happy Holiday • I Saw Mommy Kissing Santa Claus • I'll Be Home for Christmas • Let It Snow! Let It Snow! Let It Snow! • Little Saint Nick • Snowfall.

Prices, contents, and availability subject to change without notice.

FOR MORE INFORMATION, SEE YOUR LOCAL MUSIC DEALER, OR WRITE TO:

HAL•LEONARD® CORPORATION
7777 W. BLUEMOUND RD. P.O. BOX 13819 MILWAUKEE, WI 53213

Visit Hal Leonard online at **www.halleonard.com**

0604